S0-AWJ-100

BLUNDER!

BLUNDER!

HOW THE U.S. GAVE AWAY NAZI

SUPERSECRETS TO RUSSIA

Tom Agoston

Dodd, Mead & Company

NEW YORK

Copyright © 1985 by Tom Agoston
All rights reserved
No part of this book may be reproduced in any form
without permission in writing from the publisher.
Published by Dodd, Mead & Company, Inc.
79 Madison Avenue, New York, N.Y. 10016
Distributed in Canada by
McClelland and Stewart Limited, Toronto
Manufactured in the United States of America
Designed by Judith Lerner
First Edition

Library of Congress Cataloging in Publication Data

Agoston, Tom.
Blunder: how the U.S. gave away Nazi super-secrets to Russia.

Bibliography: p.
Includes index.
1. Defense information, Classified—German.
2. Defense information, Classified—United States.
3. Defense information, Classified—Soviet Union.
4. Kammler, Hans, 1903 or 4–   . 5. Voss, Wilhelm.
I. Title.
UB248.G3A46   1985   355.8'2'0943   84-24658
ISBN 0-396-08556-3

FOR
GENERAL CLARENCE R. HUEBNER

whose intrepid generalship took the First U.S. Infantry Division, the "Big Red One," and later the Fifth U.S. Corps, from a slender D-Day landing on Omaha Beach in Normandy to the capture of Pilsen, Czechoslovakia, the locale of the story here told, on the eve of the German capitulation in May 1945.

IN

grateful thanks for his helpful advice and background briefings on the military aspects of cold war newsbreaks, during his postwar tour of duty as Commander in Chief of the U.S. Army in Europe.

We went to Berlin in 1945, thinking only of the Russians as big, jolly, balalaika-playing fellows, who drank prodigious quantities of vodka, and liked to wrestle in the drawing room. We now know—or should know—that we are hopelessly naive. You can't do business with the Russians except on their own terms.

U.S. BRIGADIER GENERAL FRANK HOWLEY
Berlin Command

It is our good fortune . . . that the British and the Americans in their attitude towards us have still not emerged from their calf-love . . . all their slobber plays into our hands and we shall thank them for this in the next world with coals of fire . . . the whole of the free western world will burst apart like a fat squashed toad.

JOSEPH STALIN in 1945
quoted by Nikolai Tolstoy,
Stalin's Secret War

Contents

[ix]

CONTENTS

Author's Note

Library shelves are loaded with historical and technical accounts that studiously tell almost all there is to know about the *Götterdämmerung* of the Third Reich; the loyalty dilemmas of the men who rose within shoulder-rubbing distance of Hitler; and the pioneer Nazi scientists who developed the V-2 rocket, paving the way for the intercontinental, conventional, and nuclear missiles that today contribute to the nightmare of a space-age star war.

This is not intended to be that type of book. Nonetheless, inclusion of some of this background has been necessary, to provide the backdrop for this never-before-told story. In May 1945, as the Iron Curtain was about to be rung down across Europe, a U.S. Army combat officer in a remote corner of the collapsing Reich naively, and contrary to strictest U.S. directives, handed over the nest egg of Nazi Germany's long-range military research to the Red Army. The secrets, developed by the SS for a projected Greater-Greater Reich, provided the Soviets with an incalculable boost to their then still-trailing military research and development. The naivete that prevailed at the time has had a lasting impact.

Washington has resolutely suppressed all attempts to probe the story for almost four decades.

A parallel four-decade mystery is the simultaneous disappearance, on the eve of the collapse, of Hitler's most

trusted, all-powerful aide, the Reich's missile and jet aircraft Supremo, who had himself set up the undercover SS
operation and who was privy to all the lost research secrets and their potential to the Soviets.

The curtain is raised on both subjects for the first time.

TOM AGOSTON
Hamburg, 1984

Acknowledgments

Those who routinely work with archives invariably observe the golden rule that one should never, ever, send archivists on a "fishing expedition." Yet, in researching this book, I was amazed to find that many archivists went out of their way to find hidden pools of information, the existence of which I had been totally unaware.

This was all the more appreciated as some of the material that I sought meant probing archives on both sides of the Iron Curtain and the Atlantic, in West and East Germany, the United States, Britain, Austria, Switzerland and Egypt.

I am especially in the debt of the following: Frau Hedwig Singer of the German Federal Archives at Koblenz, whose encyclopedic knowledge of the whereabouts of material on Third Reich armament minister, the late Albert Speer, was invaluable in tracing long-forgotten documents relating to the Skoda Armament Works at Pilsen, Czechoslovakia; Herr Wilhelm Albinus, of the German Federal Military Archives at Freiburg, for unearthing unpublished documents on SS General Hans Kammler; Frau Gisela Eckert, head archivist of the former Krupp and Skoda affiliate, Salzgitter AG; Mr. Daniel P. Simon; head of the U.S. Document Center, U.S. Mission Berlin, for background material on SS General Kammler; Mr. Keith H. Jantzen, archivist of the Hoover Institution of Stanford, California, for culling the private archives of Reichoführer SS Heinrich Himmler, co-mentor with Hitler, of General Kammler and for selecting an exchange of letters between Himmler and Kammler and other relevant documents; Mr. Philip H. Reed of the Imperial War Museum Archives in London, for making available postwar U.S. interrogation reports, recorded at Nuremberg, of former Skoda president Dr. Wilhelm Voss, untraceable at the U.S. National Archives in Washington, and for providing copies of two 1945 British technical intelligence reports on the Skoda Works; Mr. Nicholas Cox of the Public Record Office in London, for scanning considerable material for relevant information; the various departments and divisions of the U.S. National Archives in Washington, for doing their best to provide unpublished material and unindexed information within the framework of the oversensitive ground rules of the U.S. government information policy that exists even for material one expects to be made available under the thirty-year rule of the U.S. Freedom of Information Act; Frau Petra Seidel of the Hamburg State University Library and her team; Frau Christiane Schaffer of the Amerika Haus Library at Hamburg and her staff; the libraries and librarians of the German Armed Forces Staff College at Blankenese, Hamburg, and the university libraries of Hanover and Munich.

Invaluable help was also forthcoming from the following: the German Red Cross, Herr Director Emanuel Witter, and the Austrian Red Cross, Herr Robert Petertill, both providing documentation and background material; West Pointer Colonel Truman E. Boudinot, Jr. of Honolulu and his brother Lieutenant Colonel Burton E. Boudinot of Radcliffe, Kentucky, for kindly supplying private photos of the Nazi concentration and labor camp Dora; Captain Johann H. Fehler, German Navy retired, World War II commander of the *U-234* submarine; Herr Herbert Gurr, attorney at law, Unna, Ruhr, for background material on General Kammler; the late Frau Irmgard Hansen of Munich for providing background material on Dr. Wilhelm Voss; William Hicklin, U.S. Army, public affairs officer of the U.S. Military Academy, West Point, NY, for helping trace the family of the late General Boudinot; Nabila Megalli, foreign correspondent, Cairo; Madame Lydia Osswald, foreign correspondent, Zürich; the late Franz von Papen, Jr., legal adviser to Dr. Voss during his attendance at Nuremberg and Frankfurt as an expert witness on Skoda; State Prosecutor A. Plitt of Arnsberg and State Prosecutor B. Tönges of Hagen, for kindly supplying relevant court records linked to General Kammler; Herr Gustav von Schmoller, Skoda expert and author, who had kindly supplied key material on Skoda and Dr. Voss; the late William Schott, retired U.S. diplomat, who recalled the wartime Berlin scene until 1941, and that his predictions of things to come, highlighted in the offical U.S. embassy diary at the time, were ignored; Herr Helmut Thöle, publisher of the Waffen SS veteran's journal *Der Freiwillinge;* Herr Wolfgang Vopersal, search service of the veterans organization of former Waffen SS members, for opening the files on Kammler; and Herr Egon von Wolmer, Munich, a former Skoda executive in Prague until 1945.

My special gratitude and thanks also go out to two World War II aides of General Kammler, who have asked for anonymity.

My gratitude and thanks are due to Mr. Eduard Linpinsel, veteran journalist, who is equally at home in the media jungles of New York and Germany, for his unstinting help, editorial advice, and arduous work in scanning the manuscript; and Mr. Denis G. Shephard, whose advice and suggestion for the inclusion and background of relevant material has much contributed to focusing light on some aspects of the story for those unfamiliar with the technical background of the narrative.

Last but very much not least, my grateful thanks to my

wife, Isabel Cogan, who applied her scripting background to ensure continuity, and whose healthy skepticism has provided an extra protective shield during interviews and, generally, during the long period of research.

BLUNDER!

TWO "PRINCES"
OF THE SS

> Leaving a battle alive after your chief
> had fallen—that meant a lifelong in-
> famy and shame.
>
> TACITUS

As OF MAY 1945, Germany was on the threshold of an open-ended period, without a flag, national anthem, or government. It was a collapse without precedent: unconditional surrender; incontestable military annihilation on land, in the air, on the sea; suspension of sovereignty; and complete occupation by four separate armies and military government teams that represented at least two totally different political and economic ideologies and aims. It conjured up the *Kaiserlose schreckliche Zeit*—the terrible interregnum without an Emperor of the thirteenth century— when the proud German royal line of Hohenstaufen suddenly became extinct in 1268 with the beheading of King Conrad IV's son, Conradine, in Italy.

The pitiless introspective confrontation with their own past the Germans were to go through in the following years was yet to come. Hitler's suicide on April 30, 1945, had knocked the props from under his planned 1,000-year Reich 988 years before the life expectancy Nazi political actuarians had conjured up for it.

[1]

In March 1945, American troops trailblazed the subsequent mass crossings of the Rhine, and the war began to rage inside the borders of the Reich. Since then Nazi propaganda for home consumption had totally lost its credibility, and the signs of the coming inevitable collapse could no longer be concealed. The accepted definition of national greatness had suddenly lost its validity. The hard fact had been brought home to the defeated people that the unpredictability of which Germany had been accused over the centuries would now apply to their own future.

No one could have foreseen that, three decades later, the free half of truncated Germany would pride itself on the predictability of its foreign policy. Its leaders, in a compulsive demonstration of a Nibelungen-type loyalty, would never tire of reiterating this in Moscow, Washington, London, Paris, Brussels, and during televised debates of the Bonn Parliament. Had the cartoonists of the Swiss satirical *Nebelspalter* or *Punch* ventured to project the specter of a new generation of German youths back in military uniform by the 1950s, goose-stepping to the Nazi pattern in East Germany and busy learning English words of command in American-style uniform and helmets in the Western half of the former Reich, they would probably have been accused of gross fantasizing.

As total chaos dawned on the eroding Reich after Hitler's suicide, two members of the elite, state-within-the-state SS—*Schutzstaffel*, rated as princes by that establishment—faced a choice. As Teutonic tradition would have it, they could follow their leader into death, or they could survive, as the symbols of the legendary phoenix.

Both had the right to wear the midnight-black and silver ceremonial uniform of the corps, displaying the dreaded twin initials in the letters of the runic alphabet. Both had immediate access to Hitler, to Reich leader of the SS Heinrich Himmler, Armaments and War Production Minister Albert Speer, and others. All corridors of power were open to them until the end. Now most of the doors to that power—including the ornate portals of the Reich Chancellory above the bunker where Hitler had lived out his final days—had been blasted out of their frames.

Yet the names of *SS Obergruppenführer* ("General") and Waffen SS General *Dr. Ing.* ("Doctor Engineer") Hans Kammler, 42, and Dr. Wilhelm Voss, 49, only made Nazi party news. Not one in a million members of the public would ever have heard of them. Both had celebrity rating in the SS. It came with their jobs. They were both members of the new aristocracy of the talented, the famous, the nation's most skilled practitioners of intrigue at the interface between their jobs, the party, the SS, and the inside clique.

The two represented a microcosm of Nazi leadership. Kammler, a rabidly nationalistic career officer, was typified by a *Tierischer Ernst*, an "awful seriousness." He was in the habit of writing wheedling letters to Reich leaders. One he signed in his characteristic way when he was already at the top.

Heil Hitler!
Your most obedient Dr. Engineer Kammler.
SS-Gruppenführer and Lieutenant General of the
Waffen SS
Commissioner of the Reichsführer-SS to the Reich minister for Armaments and War Production, Jaegerstab
[Fighter Plane Committee]

Voss, prominent cosmopolitan, top industrialist, and president of the Skoda Armament Works in German-run Czechoslovakia, had made it to the top before the war had sucked him into the maelstrom of party politics and the inevitable rank of *Standertenführer* ("colonel") in the General SS.

Now both were out of a job. Their previous positions had

made them automatic arrestees, exposed to immediate detention, interrogation, and a possible noose around their necks, if they were found guilty of war crimes as they would be defined under the ground rules of the four-power International Military Tribunal (IMT) at Nuremberg.

Kammler, the younger of the two, was regarded by many in the Nazi hierarchy as the most powerful man in Germany outside the Cabinet. He shot from the relative obscurity of a construction engineer for the Luftwaffe into top-level troubleshooting, both for Hitler and Himmler. By war's end Hitler had concentrated more power in Kammler's hands than he had ever entrusted to a single person. He even gave him authority to arrest anyone, regardless of rank, who interfered in the execution of any order he had issued.

Kammler had won his spurs by his long run of successes and by realizing never-before-tried, seemingly impossible projects, at speeds not before thought possible. His ruthless enforcement of draconic measures, regardless of the sacrifice in human effort and other people's careers, were legendary. His high academic rating of doctor engineer was a valuable asset in the 1930s, when engineering attracted the nation's best brains and served as a door opener to industry, the services, and a party career.

Kammler was reportedly attached for a time to the Soviet armed forces in the Soviet Union before World War I, when the general staffs of the two countries cooperated. The cooperation continued until 1941, when Hitler invaded the Soviet Union. Kammler's party record, on file at the United States-run Berlin Document Center,[1] omits reference to such an attachment.

With his intellectual background and fitting in with the cadre of brilliant engineers and industrialists who traditionally ran Germany, Kammler found it easy to handle the mediocre, extremely narrow-minded party types who held rank, but totally lacked the skills needed to run the economy. A modern day management consultant who was talent hunting for a "total professional with total involvement" would certainly have been fascinated by the bizarre *curriculum vitae* Kammler could have submitted. He could demonstrate a "track record" in "very senior appointments," with skill in putting across "aggressive growth plans."

If Kammler had lived in ancient Egypt, snobbish pharaohs, anxious to outshine previous dynasties, would undoubtedly have turned to him to build their pyramids. In the Rome of the Caesars, he would have been celebrated as the builder of the Coliseum, where superstar gladiators vied for the thumbs-up of crowds of 50,000.

In the Third Reich, within a span of a few years, the number of positions he had held in turn was phenomenal.

1. He had been in operational command of the indiscriminate V-rocket terror campaign of 1944 on London, Paris, Liege, Brussels, Antwerp and a number of other cities in Britain and on the Continent. To do the job he was upgraded from brigadier general to lieutenant general in one swoop.

2. He had command of the entire missile production and development program and, with it, control of the traiblazing engineers who had developed the V-2 rocket. The V-2 was the world's first long-range guided missile and ancestor of all post-war missile systems and spaceship-lifting rockets.

3. Kammler built the world's first bombproof underground aircraft and missile factory sites, including the Nordhausen plant in the Harz Mountains where thousands of his slave laborers turned out V-1 flying bombs, V-2 rockets, and engines for the Messerschmitt 262, the world's first jet fighter. This underground metropolis (eerily suggestive of the futuristic atmosphere of Fritz Lang's

science fiction film of that name) was captured undamaged by the U.S. Third Army with a bonanza of complete V-2s.

4. Kammler also commanded the SS Building and Works Division,[2] which handled building projects for the SS throughout the Greater Reich, even building roads in occupied Russia. Had Heinrich Himmler, Kammler's mentor, succeeded in building up the sovereign SS economic empire he had envisaged, utilizing a corps of 14 million forced laborers, Kammler undoubtedly would have been in command.

5. Hitler also turned to Kammler to build an underground firing range to test a scaled-down missile that would serve as a prototype for an intercontinental ballistic missile, and to prepare a feasibility study for tunneling an aircraft factory beneath a temporarily drained lake bed.

6. At the war's end, on March 27, 1945, when the Third Reich was close to collapse, Hitler appointed Kammler special plenipotentiary for speeding all modern aircraft production, specifically to get as many ME-262s into the air as possible. Believing that the superfast jet fighter could turn the tide of the war in favor of the Reich, Hitler even subordinated Goering and Speer, on their way out of Hitler's favor since 1944.

Kammler first caught the eyes of Hitler and of Himmler with a brilliant hand-colored design for the Auschwitz concentration camp, which he subsequently built. Later he was called in to advise on the modalities for boosting the daily output of its gas chambers and ovens from 10,000 to 60,000.[3]

After the uprising in the Warsaw Ghetto in 1944, it was Kammler who was assigned the task of obliterating the site. It was completely leveled, and so as to leave not a single one of the 34 million bricks,[4] Kammler's laborers recovered and moved each one from the walled-in enclave for recycling.

Kammler's last-but-one progress report was sent to Himmler on June 10, 1944, four days after Allied troops, under the supreme command of U.S. General Dwight D. Eisenhower, landed in Normandy. Marked SECRET, the report continued in the optimistic tone he routinely adopted in his communications with Himmler. It is an astounding example of the thoroughness marking his work. He went to the length of listing exactly the number of miles of rails recovered; the tonnage of iron, scrap metal, copper, brass, and lead recovered and tucked away; as well as the number and types of steam locomotives and levelers used.

It would have been inconceivable anywhere other than in the Third Reich that one man, even as brilliant as Kammler, would have been given command of as many bailiwicks, most of them in fields for which he had not been trained. If it existed in the Soviet Union today, such a position would mean that the general who commands the SS-20 rockets in Europe and Asia (the Commander in Chief of Strategic Rocket Forces) would also head research, development, and production of missiles. In addition, he would be in charge of producing all modern aircraft for the Red Air Force and have overall command of the mammoth civil engineering projects for the production centers in Siberia's subzero climate. Last, but very much not least, he would lead the national grid of gulags. To match Kammler's position in the SS, the Soviet general holding all these variegated commands would also be third in the KGB pecking order.

Existing opinions of Kammler differ widely. A senior German jurist familiar with Kammler's record describes him as the "most negatively fascinating" character of the Third Reich, the major unportrayed figure on the Nazi chessboard. His business card should have described him as *Black Genius Incarnate*.

His rival Speer wrote:

Himmler heaped assignments on him and brought him into *Hitler's presence at every opportunity.* Rumours were afloat that Himmler was trying to build up Kammler to be my successor. I had found Kammler absolutely brilliant, yet cold, a ruthless schemer, a fanatic in pursuit of his goal, as carefully calculating as he was unscrupulous.

When I first met him I rather liked his objective coolness. In many jobs my partner, in his intentions possibly my rival, he was in his career, as well as his manner of work, in many ways my *mirror image.* He too came from a solid middle class family, had gone through the University, had been "discovered" because of his work in construction and had gone far and fast in fields for which he had not been trained. No one would have thought that this quiet, unobtrusive young engineer would one day turn into one of *Himmler's most ruthless and brutal aides.* (Italics mine.)

Rocket pioneer General Walther Dornberger, who with designer Dr. Wernher von Braun developed the V-2 (after the war, von Braun was on the U.S. NASA team that put the first man on the moon), felt that Kammler's "restless piercing eyes gave one the impression of being confronted with a Renaissance *condottiere.* His mouth spelt brutality, arrogance, a powerful mouth with a protruding lip."

SS Obersturmbannführer ("Lieutenant") Rudolf Hess, first commandant of the Auschwitz concentration camp—with whom Kammler closely worked to redesign the camp's gas ovens, boosting their output—saw Kammler as "straightforward and modest in private life." Two of Kammler's wartime aides, recently interviewed, still make an idol of him.

Conflicting reports abound. A veteran American diplomat who served in Berlin until the United States entered the war in December 1941, recently recalled Kammler for the author:

> He was born to wear a uniform, but looked just as good in a custom tailored riding jacket. His love of horses and horsemanship compounded his popularity in Berlin society. But he was always unpredictable. I have seen him soothe and tame a nervous unruly horse, using a magically gentle touch, and then minutes later order a negligent groom to be brutally horsewhipped. I always thought he was a man to watch. But I never saw him again. When I got back to Berlin after the war, no one I knew seemed to remember him.

Kammler was so well wired in with Himmler that there was a saying: "If you can't reach Himmler, can't reach Pohl, then try Kammler."[5] As time went on, SS brass in Germany and abroad made it a habit to "keep in" with Kammler, to the point of bearing him in mind for special gifts, usually included in the courier pouch to *SS Standartenführer* ("Colonel") Baumert, Chief of Himmler's personal staff. In 1944 there was a shipment of booty souvenirs acquired by the SS command during the Warsaw uprising of the Polish underground in August and October of that year. Sending fur rugs, objects of art, musical instruments, valuable stamps, and a coin collection, Warsaw's SS Commander included in the shipment to Himmler an exquisite set of confiscated precision drawing instruments and slide rules as a personal gift for Kammler.

That the story of Kammler's mystery-shrouded fate at war's end intertwines with that of Voss is one of the curious tricks of destiny that neither could have foreseen.

KINGDOM LOST

> "I am sorry, Herr Baron," said the
> young man not very politely, "but
> now the Amis live here."
> "Who are the Amis?"
> "The Americans: they have taken
> over your Schloss, they have even
> moved in an entire Military Head-
> quarters. I help in the kitchen."
> "That's a good job," replied the
> man. He had not seen his home for
> four years.
>
> ERNST WIECHERT,
> *Missa Sine Nomine*

EVEN IN PHYSICAL appearance Kammler and Voss
contrasted sharply. Kammler was fair, blue-eyed, ascetic-
looking, restlessly intelligent, the perfect SS elite type. Voss,
until shortly before the collapse, was the powerful president of the Skoda armament complex in Pilsen, Czechoslovakia. Overlord, under Reichmarshal Hermann Goering's authority, of this second largest armament maker in
Europe, he was tall, quietly reserved in manner, graying,
upright, and elegant, a cosmopolitan in outlook.

Voss blended in exactly with the elite of the international arms industry, whom he regularly met before the war
on both sides of the Atlantic. They met in the privacy of
boardrooms, the habitués of which had a preference for

settling their business disputes privately rather than lifting the curtain on the inside secrets of the arms trade in an open court of law. As a prominent industrialist and simultaneously head of the Central Armaments Division in the Armaments and War Production Ministry (he also held the title *Wehrwirtschaftsführer*, "War Economy Leader"), Voss rated three listings in bold type in the then-classified British World War II *Who's Who in Nazi Germany*, a vade mecum for all British, U.S., and Allied intelligence services and embassies. He was listed alongside Krupp, the Reich's traditional arms maker; aircraft tycoons Messerschmitt and Heinkel; Porsche, the father of the Volkswagen; and coal and steel magnate Flick. As head of a department at the Speer ministry, he rated a separate entry. Then there is a thumbnail biography.

At war's end Voss had been out of a job since January 27, 1945, when Goering dismissed him from all offices (Goering headed the Hermann Goering Werke, the industrial empire to which Skoda belonged), even barring him from the Skoda site. The problem was Voss's refusal to appoint two of the Reichmarshal's "special envoys" to the Skoda management, and party differences. Voss had joined Skoda in 1938, when the plant was ceded to the Reich under the Munich Pact—Hitler, Chamberlain, Mussolini, and Daladier, allotting the Sudeten German areas of Czechoslovakia to Germany—and became an affiliate of Hitler's principal arms maker Krupp.[1] With his flair for quiet diplomacy, Voss was immensely popular with the Czech executives, who had remained in leading positions at the time of the German takeover of Skoda. Voss even saw to it that Czech workers, paid on the local and not Reich wage scales, were paid more money.

By quirk of fate, the careers of Kammler and Voss overlapped at Skoda, where they jointly set up and operated what was generally regarded by insiders as the Reich's most advanced high-technology military research center. Working as a totally independent undercover operation for the SS, the center was under the special auspices of Hitler and Himmler. Going outside the scope and field of Skoda's internationally coveted general research and development division, it worked closely with Krupp and was primarily concerned with analysis of captured equipment, including aircraft, and copying or improving the latest technical features. In so doing the SS group was to go beyond the first generation of secret weapons.

Its purpose was to pave the way for building nuclear-powered aircraft, working on the application of nuclear energy for propelling missiles and aircraft; laser beams, then still referred to as "death rays"; a variety of homing rockets; and to seek other potential areas for high-technology breakthrough. In modern high-tech jargon, the operation would probably be referred to as an "SS research think tank." Some work on second-generation secret weapons, including the application of nuclear propulsion for aircraft and missiles, was already well advanced.

It was far from a mad Nazi scientist's dream of getting to the end of the nuclear rainbow. The field had been pioneered by Dr. Wernher von Braun, designer of the V-2, in the early 1930s. In addition, it was recently disclosed that one of the first top German engineers cleared for urgent work for the U.S. Air Force in 1945 was Dr. Franz Josef Neugebauer, a specialist in thermal systems for aircraft nuclear propulsion.[2] In 1958 the United States launched Project Orion to probe the applicability of nuclear propulsion for aircraft, employing some Czech scientists. The project was continued until 1965 and then was turned over to the U.S. Air Force, plans for its application for the civilian space programs having been dropped.

The SS research operation at Skoda had been set up without the knowledge of Goering, Speer, or the German research centers. The builders of the V-1 and the V-2 were likewise kept out of the picture. The undercover SS research operation fitted in with Himmler's dream that, as the Rheingold of the Nibelung's, if shaped into a ring, would give its possessor mastery of the world, so would the SS team give the Greater-Greater Reich mastery of much of the world.

A study of intelligence reports shows that blueprints, drawings, calculations, and other relevant documentation or materials were protected by a triple ring of SS counter-intelligence specialists Himmler had assigned to Pilsen to prevent security leaks and sabotage in the research divisions and the plant in general. The SS team was internally referred to as the Kammler Group. Taking a leaf from the armament ministry name for the special section Kammler headed there to iron out aircraft production bottlenecks, they were called the Kammler *stab* or Kammler "staff."[3]

The funding for the Pilsen SS operation was channeled through Voss, who thus was able to remain in the picture, as he recalled when describing the setup to me in Frankfurt in 1949.

In the course of several extended interviews in Frankfurt and at his home in Bavaria, Voss spoke of his past activities with unique frankness.

Skoda's overtly operating research and development division, working closely with the SS group on some projects, had provided a convenient cover for the Kammler Group specialists, culled in great secrecy from Germany's research institutes to supplement the in-house experts. All were picked for their know-how and not their party records, Voss said. All had to have the ability to tackle visionary projects. A number were Czech nationals. Some had worked in the United States before the war.

Working for the Kammler project had provided new opportunities for the experts. Traditionally German industry had always concentrated on high-quality research to provide saleable, up-to-date, beautifully engineered products. Successful sales drives helped boost the arms industry. Circumvention of the restrictive terms of the Versailles Treaty and the limits set on warship and aircraft production served as an incentive to produce equipment with a far bigger punch. Many scientists, anxious to see their work in print, even if it was kept top secret, prepared papers for a central office of scientific reports, which circulated them to specific recipients. Some of these reports were used as the basis for selecting candidates for employment at Skoda.

Himmler put top priority on routing all Waffen SS research and weapons development contracts to Skoda and regarded smooth cooperation between the Waffen SS armaments office and Skoda of utmost importance. This is reflected in correspondence between Voss and Himmler. To ensure this cooperation, Himmler set up a Waffen SS liaison unit at Skoda, putting Voss in charge. Voss reported directly to Himmler.

Voss recalled that the Reich armament hierarchy was initially very reluctant to treat Skoda on an equal footing with Krupp and other "real German" armament firms, possibly regarding the formerly-Austrian, later-Czech Skoda as "foreign." According to a veteran German general staffer, the hesitation of the Waffen SS brass to treat Skoda on an equal footing with German firms may well have been rooted in an estimate of the future military situation by some seasoned generals. To them, the worsening military situation on the eastern front by late 1941 and early 1942 forecast the possibility of an Allied victory and the unavoidable linkup of the Red Army with the Western Allied armies somewhere in Central Europe, most likely the Slav part of Czechoslovakia. To these generals, this meant only one thing—the loss of Skoda's records and sectors enriched over eight years with Krupp know-how, to the Soviets.

Such long-term appreciation of the situation would have been a normal product of staff exercises staged by the increasingly nervous German General Staff. To them the erratic, and more and more tragic, strategic decisions of their Austrian-born, German militarist *feldherr* (Commander in Chief) presented a nagging problem. Hitler, to whom the possibility of defeat was just "not on," directed that Skoda should immediately be treated on full equal footing with German firms, also in regard to secret equipment. This was spelled out in the minutes of the Führer Conference of March 15, 1942, with Reinhard Heydrich. Subsequently assassinated, Heydrich was their head of the SS Security Service (RSHA) and Reich Protector of Bohemia and Moravia, the former being the Czech province in which the Skoda Works are located.

Just how right the old-school Prussian generals were became increasingly clear by 1944, when the Allied terms for the future carving-up of Europe were arrived at in Yalta. For Voss, the inevitability that Skoda, with its potential for the Soviet war economy, would fall into Soviet hands was a nightmare. And, since his dismissal by Goering in January 1945, he was powerless to take steps to intervene in any way.

THREE

KAMMLER'S METROPOLIS

I tell you why the Nazis were so *mächting* (powerful) in Germany: because, as any *Dummkopf* (fool) knows, it is the best thing in life to have one boss, and then to stop thinking and just do everything he tells you to do.

BERLIN TAXI DRIVER IN 1945,
QUOTED BY TONI HOWARD IN *Shriek
with Pleasure.*

THE FLOCK OF WILD Harz canaries in the boughs of the trees lining the mountain road in the heart of Saxony were quick to react to the unfamiliar pitch of the rumbling Sherman tanks of Combat Command B (CCB) of the U.S. Third Armored Division. The roar of the rolling armor drove them in shrill alarm to less noisy parts.

CCB was on a reconnaissance to investigate local rumors that there were unusual things at nearby Nordhausen. Unconfirmed British intelligence reports had suggested that the Nazi's long-sought, secret, bombproof underground V-weapon and jet engine production center was located somewhere in the Harz. But neither the RAF nor U.S. air reconnaissance had been able to pinpoint it.[1] The local tip was of paramount tactical and strategic importance and appeared to indicate that the U.S. column, on the move since it had landed at Normandy, was very close to the site.

The German General Staff had been aware of the very rapid advance of General George Patton's one-half-million-strong army and made the preemptive move during the last week of March 1945 to order Kammler to evacuate some 500 handpicked rocket designers and technicians from Nordhausen to Oberammergau in Bavaria. They added the totally impracticable rider that the group "resume" research, even though there was no doubt in anyone's mind that it was to be the Reich's eleventh hour.

Kammler used the opportunity to get out of Berlin and set up his operations in Munich, which he regarded as more central for his various activities. He was much embittered by having to evacuate Nordhausen and by knowing it would inevitably be captured, by whichever of the opposing forces reached it first. He had regarded the project as one of the most important jobs—if not *the* most important—he had ever handled. It was tangible proof that he could manage anything he had set his mind to. Ironically the credit for putting the aircraft factories underground went to Speer, who initially regarded it as impossible. Even the official German weekly newsreel released on Wednesday, May 3, 1944, featuring work in progress for underground factory projects, credited Speer and overlooked Kammler's major role.

The V-2 production project—which Hitler regarded vital for the overall plan to prevent the Western Allied cross-Channel invasion—had been dogged ever since the massive RAF Bomber Command raid on Peenemunde, the original site of the V-2 production, the previous year. On August 17, 1943, RAF Bomber Command Commander in Chief Sir Arthur Harris threw 571 bombers into attack.

Despite very heavy RAF losses, the raid paid off. It succeeded in destroying most of the V-2 construction blueprints as they were about to be handed to the workshops, the summit of all research and experimental work. The destruction delayed the first scheduled use of the V-2s from early 1944, the eve of the projected invasions, until September 1944, thus directly contributing to the success of the Allied landings in Normandy on June 6, 1944.

String-pulling within the power-hungry SS and all the good will that was going for Kammler at the Chancellory put him into command at Peenemunde soon after the RAF raid, and he was in physical command by September. In a rare exhibition of diplomacy, Kammler retained Army Colonel Dr. Walther Dornberger as second in command, a factor that was to become decisive in the future of the cream of the Peenemunde group, after its surrender to the U.S. Army in May, 1945.

There was no doubt in the Western Allied camp that, ever since the Luftwaffe had lost its aerial superiority in 1943—with no sign of retaining it, despite the appearance of the superfast, trailblazing ME-262 jet fighter—success or failure of the Allied invasion hinged on General Kammler's ability to muster enough rockets to destroy the Allied invasion ports before the Continent-bound armadas could form up. Writing in his *Crusade of Europe*, General Dwight D. Eisenhower was brutally frank about the narrow escape and the very thin thread upon which the fate of Europe hinged: "If the Germans had succeeded in perfecting and using these new weapons six months before they did, the Normandy landings might have proved exceedingly difficult, perhaps impossible. If they had made the Portsmouth-Southampton area their principal targets, Overlord might have been written off."

This assessment prompted Allied military commanders, even Ike's critics, to regard it necessary to eliminate at once the menace of the V-weapons—first heralded by an anon-

ymous well-wisher to British Intelligence in Oslo in 1939—
not only to protect civilian life and property, but equally
to prevent interference with Allied military operations.

Most historians agree that had Hitler put the superfast
twin turbojet Messerschmitt 262 fighter (initially known
as Messerschmitt Project 1065: ME P 1065) into production immediately after it was first test-flown on July 18,
1942, its early operational deployment would undoubtedly
have changed the course of the war.

The delay was partly attributed to Hitler's meddlesome
and amateurish insistence on ordering the upgrading of the
embryo ME-262 fighter into a bomber codenamed 262-A-
Sturmvogel (Stormbird). The project was later dropped, but
the error could no longer be rectified.

The first ME-262 only entered combat service on July 10,
1944, one month after the Normandy landings, by which
time Allied air superiority completely swamped the Luftwaffe.

(For the record: the ME-262 was not the world's first
turbojet-powered fighter: Heinkel's HE-280 was test-flown
on April 2, 1941, more than a year before the ME-262 was
first put through its paces, but the project was subsequently discontinued.)

Apart from his move to Bavaria, which had attracted
minimum attention at the SS economic and administrative main office in Berlin, Kammler told confidants he felt
personally uprooted in more ways than one. The wide range
of blanket powers he had exercised over several years,
capped by his recent promotion at Hitler's hands as plenipotentiary for all rocket and modern jet aircraft production, had begun to erode. With it went his privately nur-
tured dream of emerging as the savior of the Reich,
protecting the state as a modern-day Mars, with a Pan-
dora's box of secrets at his disposal.

The unexpected diversion of the main U.S. and British

thrust from the road to Berlin into a new drive toward the rich German provinces of Saxony and Thuringia puzzled Kammler as it did the German General Staff, who expected a main thrust to get to Berlin before the Red Army did. To Allied troops, the diversion to the east and south had come as a surprise and disappointment. The motivation and grounds for the new battle plan eluded them. Ever since D-Day, when the taking of Berlin was held out to them as one of the principal objectives of Operation Overlord, they had been counting the days and miles that stood between them and the capital of the hated Reich. They looked forward to symbolically sitting astride it as conquerors. This was what every fighting man had longed to experience. This was the story the folks at home wanted to hear, and they were mindful of their hometown papers.

Now these troops, who a few days before were only some sixty miles from Berlin, found themselves closing in on the legend-rich Harz Mountains. From there the Czechoslovakian border, their assigned easternmost limit, was only an easy day's ride. The totally rewritten Allied battle scenario and the surprise it had brought to both the Allied commands that rounded off the American continent and the German side also introduced a totally new dimension into the Kammler story.

The need for rescripting had been rooted in the suddenly stiffened German resistance of nine months before, which forced the gallop of the converging Allied thrusts to slow into a slow trot. The previous September things still looked good for the West. The Allies had crossed into the Reich near Aachen, and the Red Army, the largest standing army in history, had driven the Germans out of Russia and back onto Reich territory.

Suddenly the supposedly wise and prudent generals and statesmen in the West, who had pinned high hopes on seeing an early end to the blood and desolation of war, found themselves having to rescale the wall they believed they had long since surmounted.

The thrust through France had petered out, dashing "Forever Lucky" Patton's hopes for a quick, decisive breakthrough at Metz. He was suddenly frustrated by bad luck, as was Field Marshal Bernard Montgomery. Monty's spectacular 1942 defeat of the "Desert Fox," Field Marshal Erwin Rommel, and his Africa Corps seemed far off now, as he failed to outflank the Siegfried line for a clear run through to Berlin. The Luftwaffe bit back with a vengeance. Their superfast Messerschmitt 262s, the world's first-ever jet fighters, were playing havoc with the much slower conventional American and British fighters. U.S. President Franklin D. Roosevelt and British Prime Minister Winston Churchill began to send confidential briefs to their governments, warning that "no one knows when the war will be finished" and directing their military and civilian officials to refrain from suggesting that the "end of the war is in sight."[2]

The American advance into Saxony and Thuringia, which were conquered with the loss of thousands of American lives, was one of the first Allied successes of early 1945. The subsequent pullout from the two provinces, under a vague barter deal with the Soviets, embittered Americans in the combat zone and at home. "The Russians were taking over our territory of Saxony and Thuringia, crops, cattle, castles, marble baths, wild ducks and all," wrote U.S. Brigadier General Frank Howley, first U.S. commandant of the military government team in the U.S. sector of the former Reich capital.[3]

The factor that most worried the Allied commands was a sudden flow, as of March 1945, of U.S. intelligence reports from the Office of Strategic Services (OSS, forerunner of the Central Intelligence Agency, CIA). They reported that the Germans were preparing an "armed and defended Alpine National Redoubt" in "Southern Germany and Northern Austria," to enable Nazi leaders to "carry on the fight." According to OSS reports, the "Redoubt" was to be defended by "most sophisticated secret weapons and elite troops, trained to organize the Reich's resurrection and liberation of Germany from the Occupying forces." The "Redoubt" was said to have its operational command near Salzkammergut in Austria and its supreme command at Obersalzberg, Hitler's retreat near Berchtesgaden.

The "National Redoubt" in fact never existed. It proved to be nothing more than a propaganda myth. Yet the Allies accepted the OSS reports at their face value. The misjudgment not only swept away the basic target of Overlord, it also created a political running sore and flashpoint at the most critical interface between East and West in Europe. Ultimately, it contributed to a basic change in the face of Europe.

Today, with the specter of total nuclear war looming between the two superpowers that joined forces almost four decades ago to defeat Nazi Germany, the record of events that April 1945 reveals an alarming degree of political naiveté. And the naifs were plentiful on both sides of the Atlantic.

From March onward, the OSS report had taken hold to an extent that they began to influence Allied tactical thinking. By the spring of 1945, the myth of a "National Redoubt" had rapidly mushroomed among the military, despite the caveats from British and U.S. military intelligence.

The official kill-off of Berlin as an objective came from General Omar Bradley's Twelfth Army group. In an uncompromising top secret memorandum, Bradley announced that the significance of Berlin had "much diminished" and that the metropolitan area was "no longer a position of importance." The memo climaxed in the historic statement that the "reorientation of Allied objectives had rendered obsolete plans we have brought with us over the beaches."[4]

On April 11, Eisenhower finally decided to abandon the idea of taking Berlin, even though it was known to be thinly defended, and the Red Army was nowhere near the Reich capital. He ordered Montgomery, less than sixty miles from Berlin, to divert to the south and east as part of a crash program to divide Germany into two halves, so as to deny German troops the chance of flooding into the "Redoubt" area.

Contrary to the belief generally accepted in the first wave of postwar political postmortems, which claimed that Eisenhower's sudden strategy switch had been based on fresh intelligence data, documentation in the possession of the author shows without a shadow of doubt that the "Redoubt" phantom had been planted four months previously. Once again the information source was the OSS.

There appears to be no evidence that Allied military leaders had taken steps to probe the validity of the early OSS reports, despite their ponderous implications.[5] The earlier OSS intelligence forecast, the first to mention the "Redoubt" complex, was published by the analysis branch of the OSS on December 29, 1944. The report, marked CLASSIFIED, was keynoted by the prediction that "the Germans would probably establish reduits [sic] when the fighting has stopped."

It continued:

The heart of the plan would probably be a *reduit,* a mountain strongpoint, fortified and provisioned in advance, defended by strong guerrilla garrisons, serving as a base for marauding guerrilla bands. From such retreats the Nazis would probably be able to prolong resistance

[23]

BLUNDER!

for a considerable time. . . . It would be unwise to rule
out that from some top party Chieftains, probably too
well known to disappear underground, the *reduit* would
provide the stage for a spectacular last stand fight.

Subsequent events showed that the "Redoubt" had no
more substance than the deception operations the Wehrmacht routinely used. They continuously circulated rumors about the pending arrival of fictitious reinforce-
ments, rapidly changing dummy headquarters and "advance
personnel," even putting inflatable rubber tanks in the field
to deceive photo interpreters. These were the types of rumors that the OSS should have analyzed and scotched, instead of disseminating them over a period of several months,
thereby influencing military and political strategy to the
benefit of the Soviet Union. Eisenhower's command decision to seize the "Redoubt" before the Nazis could organize it for defense was knocked into a cocked hat when
Allied troops discovered that the "Redoubt" was a phantom. It was no more than a composite of unimplemented
proposals submitted to Hitler by Nazi fanatics in Bavaria,
and was subsequently shown to be a realistic *ruse-de-guerre*
furthered by the disinformation experts of Propaganda
Minister Josef Goebbels, who targeted leaks to neutral correspondents in Berlin. The Goebbels-huckstered ruse had
taken such deep root within the Allied Supreme Command that correspondents at Supreme Headquarters, Allied Expeditionary Force (SHAEF), including myself, were
actually shown an Allied map purporting to mark Nazi
military dispositions within the "Redoubt." Bradley, later
chief of the U.S. Joint Chiefs of Staff, had to concede shortly
after the war that:

. . . not until the campaign ended were we to learn that
this Redoubt existed largely in the imagination of a few
fanatic Nazis. It grew into so exaggerated a scheme that

I am astonished that we could have believed it as inno-
cently as we did. But while it persisted, this legend of
the Redoubt was too ominous a threat to ignore, and in
consequence it shaped our tactical thinking during the
closing weeks of the war.[6]

Just how important this last-minute change of strategy
proved to be was shortly demonstrated. Soon Berlin and all
major Eastern European capitals were within the Soviet orbit. As Winston Churchill underscored with bitter emphasis, "Soviet Russia was established in the heart of Europe.
This was a fateful milestone for mankind." Churchill's
foreboding followed in the wake of Lenin's prophesy that
"he who holds Berlin, is Lord of Europe and thus of the
world."

John J. McCloy, the first U.S. High Commissioner of the
post-military era, inherited the problem of guaranteeing non-
existent accords on completely free access to Berlin. He
sadly remarked later: "Any number of people should have
thought of this situation, irrespective of their particular responsibility. If anyone did think of it he certainly held his
peace. I certainly wish I had thought of it or taken some
responsibility even if I didn't have it. I think the same thing
can be said of all those who were involved with. . . our
overall European policy, and I include the President, the
Chief of Staff, Eisenhower, Clay, the Secretary of State, the
Secretary of War . . ."[7]

By the same year Eisenhower was clearly embarrassed by
his 1945 assessment of the Russians and his failure to take
Berlin. Professor Stephen Ambrose of the University of New
Orleans, writing in his comprehensive book *Eisenhower*,[8]
stated in part:

In various ways he tried to rewrite the historical record,
asserting in his memoirs references to this or that warning he gave to this or that politician about the Russians.

[25]

He may well have uttered such warnings but he did not mention them in *Crusade in Europe* (1948), nor in *At Ease* (1967), nor did he ever write anything during the war to indicate that he was fearful of Russian intentions. . . . When he claimed to have done so it was noticeable that in both cases he said he made his point in private, and in both cases the man who he made it to, was dead.

The gross, irreversible political blunder over Berlin and the trump cards the Western policymakers have left in the Soviet's hands continue to overshadow all East-West talks over Europe, especially issues involving the two Germanies and Eastern Europe.

This was dramatically underscored by U.S. President Ronald Reagan in his speech in Normandy on June 7, 1984, commemorating the fortieth anniversary of the D-Day landings:

Countries that were to be liberated by the Allies, were later lost to Soviet occupation. The great sadness of this loss echoes down to our own times in the streets of Warsaw, Prague, and East Berlin . . . Soviet troops that came to the center of this continent did not leave when peace came.

It had soon began to dawn on the Western Allies that Eisenhower's decision to yield Berlin to the Soviets before the Anglo-American forces had a chance to seize it was one of the worst military/political blunders of the war—if not *the* worst.[9] Whether or not the "National Redoubt" bogey was a cleverly orchestrated piece of Soviet disinformation, meant to divert the Anglo-American forces from taking Berlin before the Red Army could get there, will remain an open question.

Machinery for planting disinformation with the OSS was

provided through the close wartime links between the Soviet NKVD (forerunner of the KGB, Committee for State Security), the OSS, and British intelligence to the point that the three agencies exchanged information.[10] There were parallel links between NKVD and the Gestapo through its chief, General Heinrich Mueller (Gestapo Mueller). After seeing Hitler in the Berlin bunker on April 29 1945, the day before Hitler committed suicide, Mueller dropped out of sight. Nevertheless, German prisoners of war in Russia later reported seeing him alive and active in Moscow.

Soviet infiltration of German government agencies and services before, during, and after World War II subsequently made headlines. In 1977, the disclosure that Chancellor Willy Brandt's political aide Guenther Guillaume, who had access to NATO secrets and was a major figure in Communist East German intelligence, toppled Brandt from office.[11] The sudden switch in Allied planning—not to take Berlin, but to search for a redoubt that did not exist—brought at least one bonanza. The rapid eastward drive of the U.S. Third Army brought it to Kammler's secret metropolis well ahead of the Russians in whose designated zone it lay. The Nordhausen bonanza proved to be one of the greatest technical prizes in history.

It was only by fluke that Combat Command B found the Reich's sole remaining rocket factory. Under Kammler's instructions, the factory remained operational even after the evacuation of some 500 representative members of the operation to Oberammergau. The clue that CCB had hit the right spot came with the discovery of a number of V-2 rockets stacked at the entrance to a tunnel leading to the plant. At last the first of the Western Allies had reached the long-sought, last-ditch Reich missile and jet engine production plant that had been turning out the reprisal weapons Kammler's rocket troops used in the V-2 offensive against Britain, France, and other countries.

When CCB entered the huge plant, it found to its surprise that it was totally intact, that hundreds of completed V-1 and V-2 assemblies had been left undisturbed. The vast underground labyrinth of the underground factory Kammler had designed was the world's biggest of its kind. "There were hundreds of parts of the great V-2 rocket lying on the ground and on flatcars, standing in the siding: nose sections, central sections, tails. Surrounded by these strange devices, I felt as though I had woken in another planet," wrote American aviator Colonel Charles A. Lindbergh, who visited the plant shortly after its capture on April 11. Lindbergh, whose first nonstop solo flight from New York to Paris in May 1927 made him America's first post-World War I hero, was on the first stage of his U.S. Naval Technical Mission to study German wartime development in aircraft and missiles.

Writing in his *Wartime Diary* Lindbergh continued: "A full-size railroad track runs all the way through the tunnel. We drove past side tunnels filled with machinery, engine and rocket parts. There were miles of tunnels, some producing V-2 parts, some producing parts for Junkers engines." The vastness, the precision of Kammler's trailblazing concept of tunneling a factory into a mountain invariably drew the admiration of all who saw it.

The nearby shocking remains of the Dora concentration and extermination camps, from which Kammler drew his slave laborers for the underground factory, were discovered by another element of CCB. The camp itself was almost completely abandoned, as most of the skilled workers had been transferred to other camps on Kammler's orders. Americans entering the camp could not believe their eyes. Combat Command B commander, Brigadier General Truman E. Boudinot, was one of the first to enter the compound.[12] A member of his staff recalled the scene in the official U.S. Army history of CCB.

Hundreds of corpses lay sprawled over the acres of the big compound. More hundreds filled the great barracks. They lay in contorted heaps, half stripped, mouths gaping in the dirt and straw, or they were piled naked like cordwood.

No written word can properly convey the atmosphere of such a charnel house, the unbearable stench of the decomposing bodies. They were so far gone in the depth of starvation that death was a matter of hours. The highly efficient German *Herrenvolk* who caused the situation. . . were acting out a clearly defined program. These prisoners were political enemies of the Third Reich, Germans, Poles, Hungarians, fourteen-year-old boys and aged men, French Resistance, Belgians, Poles, Russians—a Babel of tongues dying together in the filth and dirt of their own dysentery. The prisoners had dragged themselves to work on V-1 and V-2 assembly lines, although they were starved on four ounces of black bread and a small amount of thin soup each day. They worked because the SS had a cure for slackers or alleged saboteurs. At Dora they hanged 32 men one day and forced the garrison to watch. Then the bodies were hauled to the crematorium ovens.

When news of the sensational find at Nordhausen was flashed to the ordnance corps rocket branch in Washington, which was already aware of the existence of the V-2 factory, Colonel Holger Toftoy, chief of the ordnance technical intelligence team in Paris, was directed to ship out one hundred V-2 assemblies and parts to White Sands.[13] In a subsequent analysis of captured German documents on aerodynamics by General Henry (Hap) Arnold, U.S. Joint Chief of Staff, and Professor Theodor Kármán, General Arnold stated:

We are very much behind in this development in a
number of research factors. If we do not take this opportunity, seize this equipment and the men who developed it, and fail to put them to work at once, we will
lose many years and we could be working on problems
already solved.

At the time U.S. intelligence was aware that the Soviets
had no large rockets with sizable thrust, jet aircraft, or
electrically powered submarines. The Germans had all these,
and the Soviets were known to be busy looking for proto-
types, blueprints, and experts.

At Nordhausen, U.S. ordnance technical officer Major
(later Lieutenant-General) James Hamill, assigned to prepare the rocket assemblies and jet engines for shipment to
the U.S., at once realized the technological bonanza within
reach. Under Washington's authority and by the terms of
U.S. Joint Chief of Staff Directive 1067 of April 24, 1945—
to "preserve from destruction and take under control all
records, plans, books, documents, papers, files and scientific, industrial and other information and data belonging
to German organizations engaged in military research"—
he went ahead fulfilling his assignment before the scheduled handing over of the Nordhausen Mittelwerke (Central Works) to the Red Army.

Kammler's metropolis remained in American hands for
ten more weeks before the Red Army was able to reach it.
Exactly four weeks after Nordhausen fell to CCB, and even
before the U.S. weapons technical intelligence team was set
to start evacuating as many V-2s and turbojets from the
underground production center, the Third Reich had run
its course.

The packing, crating, and loading of the missiles and engines, the components, parts, and other material was rushed
through in a ten-day crash program. Hamill was able to ship

out 100 V-2 components and accessories to Antwerp. The cargo, weighing 400 tons, filled 314 railcars and, subsequently, 15 Liberty ships.

The evacuation of the material began on May 22, one day after Speer, undergoing interrogation by the U.S. Strategic Bombing Survey Mission at Glückstadt in north Germany, suggested that Kammler should be located for questioning in regard to the operational use of the V-2s, which he had commanded. The loading was completed on May 31, 1945.

As ten days before, when Kammler's name suddenly shot into the limelight during Speer's interrogation, the shadow of the former master of the underground metropolis also loomed at Nordhausen that day. As Hamill completed the loading of the last V-2s, which were soon on their way to the U.S., eventually to pave the way for putting the first man on the moon, he suddenly pondered whether he should put Nordhausen out of action now, before the Red Army took over.[14] As Kammler had before him, Hamill hesitated to do so and followed Kammler's example of leaving it intact.

SAMURAI CARGO

Into an ancient pool
A frog leaps—cool
The sound of water
MATSUO BASHŌ

LONG BEFORE THE WAR had reached the stage where the United States and the Soviet Union began to crate captured German V-weapons and hire the men who had developed the technology, many Japanese ordnance factories were turning out military hardware for their war economy, using Skoda-Krupp machine tools. Nazi Germany's most sensitive secrets—concerning missiles, modern aircraft, industry, science, and the military—were regularly supplied to Japan, under the noses of Washington and London. Even fissionable uranium-235 was reportedly made available to Berlin's prime Axis ally.

The full extent of this wartime transfer of Nazi secrets remains an unknown quantity, as are details of the patents exchanged between the two nations. Just as the Nazi military technology that wound up in U.S. and Soviet hands gave both nations a tremendous head start in guided missiles and other fields, the German technology transfer to Japan has provided that country with the core of its robotic and microchip technology, much of it developed from German know-how and patents.

The green light for the technological transfer was given by Hitler himself on April 4, 1941 at a meeting with visiting Japanese Foreign Minister Yosuke Matsuoka. The exchange and its aftermath was riddled with double talk and double cross, as captured German and Japanese documents show.

In 1941, both Germany and Japan were probing ways and means of splitting the British Empire. Germany wanted Japan to launch an immediate strike at Singapore, Malaya, and the Dutch East Indies. It assured Tokyo that if it moved fast, the United States would not dare move out of its corral of neutrality and make a move in the Pacific.

The German assessment of Washington's likely stand on Japanese action in Singapore and Malaya made little impact on Premier Prince Konoye and a number of senior Army and Navy officers. Konoye continued to seek reconciliation with the United States.

The military equipment and technology Japan sought in 1941 was primarily needed for completing its conquest of China. It was a far cry from the sophisticated hardware and technology shipped later. But in 1941 it helped build up Japan's image among its partners within the "Greater East-Asia Co-prosperity Sphere," which provided it with essential raw materials and markets.

U.S.-educated but anti-American Matsuoka, more ideologically pro-German than most of his Cabinet colleagues, was completely under Hitler's spell, but shared Cabinet concern over the friendship pact Hitler had concluded with Stalin three weeks after the outbreak of World War II in September 1939.

The main purpose of Matsuoka's mission to Berlin was to assess the extent of Germany's mastery of Europe by side visits to Moscow and Rome, and to learn when the much heralded invasion of Britain was likely to begin. During his talks in Berlin, Matsuoka was assured that Germany was "in the final phase of battle" against Britain, and that the Luftwaffe and its most modern air armada (it did not yet have the ME-262) would remain the unchallenged master of European air space. At their April 4 meeting Hitler even declared that he had made "ample preparations to ensure that no American would ever land in Europe." The little-known quotation surfaced in testimony at Nuremberg and appears in the trial records.

In his post-mission report to Premier Konoye, Matsuoka had highest praise for Germany's military strengths, but stressed that his German hosts had been most noncommital in regard to German-Soviet relations. They never went beyond stating that relations were normal, and they never indicated whether they intended to implement their plan to invade Britain. In Matsuoka's view, Hitler, as well as Prince Konoye, was anxious to avoid a conflict with the United States. Two months after the Matsuoka mission to Europe, Germany rocked the world by its undeclared invasion of Russia.

The eastward blitz of June 22, 1941 came as a complete shock to Japan. Matsuoka had no inkling of the aggression. The resulting loss of face directly contributed to ending his Cabinet career. The invasion of Russia did not come as a complete surprise to Stalin, whose German superspy Richard Sorge, in the entourage of the German ambassador in Tokyo, had tipped the KGB ahead of time.

The devastating Japanese attack on the U.S. Pacific Fleet in Pearl Harbor on December 7, 1941 astonished Hitler and his staff. It immediately brought home the fact that the United States was now inevitably linked with the British Empire and the Soviet Union. Events had suddenly boosted the priority rating and nature of the German technology transfer to Japan. Almost four decades later, capital-rich Japan—with its breathtaking build-up of economic prosperity that has baffled the world—is reciprocating for the generous assistance it had received from the Reich during World War II. Japan provides West Germany's parched investment scene with much-needed capital and opportunities to acquire new technologies, some originally sparked by German know-how.

The wide palette of German know-how that was made available to Japan surprised Allied technical intelligence experts when they were finally able to study captured records. Much still remains under wraps in both Germany and Japan. The shipment of Skoda-Krupp machine tools had been specially authorized by the German General Staff. The choice ranged from anti-aircraft guns (8.8- and 12.7-centimeter), naval guns (10.5- and 15-centimeter), and several varieties of the 12.7-centimeter piece.

Prior to the German invasion of the Soviet Union in 1941, some daredevil German merchant Navy skippers could rely on Soviet assistance in braving the ice off Siberia. En route to the Pacific they took the same route the German raiding cruiser *Schiff 45* used to reach the Pacific, and they captured 64,000 tons of British and Allied shipping. Blueprints of Kammler's pet Messerschmitt 262 jet fighter were also included in the Tokyo-bound technical bonanza. In September 1944, two engineers from the Junkers aircraft factory hand carried a number of blueprints to Japan.

By war's end, Germany was in the process of testing much faster ways of getting urgent cargo, spare parts, engineers, and other key service and party personnel to Tokyo. On March 28, 1945, a Luftwaffe test pilot flew a six-engine JU-390 (Junkers) long-range bomber to Japan via the Polar route, a nonstop flight of some 18,000 miles. This automatically put Japanese-controlled Manchoutikuo (the state of Manchu) within reach. But the most spectacular of all shipments ever sent to Japan left by submarine on March 30, 1945, via Norway. This was the last submarine to sail from the rapidly collapsing Reich before its capitulation. Three others, just completed for delivery to the Japanese Navy (*U-256, U-2511,* and *U-3514*), were unable to fulfill the contract and were captured when the German Navy surrendered. The vessel picked to sail to Tokyo at that late date was to take the Cape route. It meant braving the heavily patrolled Atlantic, swarming with U.S. and British naval vessels. The submarine *U-234*—a giant PXB-type, snorkel-fitted, 2,000-ton converted minelayer—was ideally suited for the job. Its specially fitted fuel tanks gave it a range of more than 20,000 miles at an average surface speed of between fourteen and sixteen knots. It had just left the Krupp fitting-out basin at Kiel.

After two postponements of the original sailing date, duly spotted and announced over the air by the British Psychological Warfare-operated "Forces Radio Calais," the *U-234* finally set off for Norway on the first leg of its journey. The vessel carried 260 tons of cargo, including a dismantled twelve-meter-long ME-262 jet fighter, jet engine components, several sealed metal drums believed to have contained jet engine blueprints (Messerschmitt and Junkers) and almost 100 tons of mercury, welded inside the outer hull, to serve as ballast. Also aboard were some 100 Leica cameras and a quantity of optical glass (possible forerunner of Japan's postwar miniature camera export drive), electronic equipment, and ammunition for the Japanese-controlled German submarine base at Penang (Malaysia). The sub also carried nine months' iron rations of food, cigarettes, spirits, and other victuals, should circumstances force the crew to abandon ship and fend for themselves.[1] The wartime influx of very advanced German know-how of optics, electronics, synthetics, and pioneering miniaturization of sophisticated guidance and other equipment—a spin-off of the German missile program—has considerably contributed to Japan's subsequent, devastatingly effective economic miracle.

Because of its top-secret assignment, its commander, Captain Johann Heinrich Fehler, did not have an inkling of what he was to carry to Tokyo. Fehler only realized that he was indeed on a "very special mission" when he was suddenly ordered to cut his crew by eighteen—"all trained men," Fehler recalled—to make room for twenty-six VIPs and other special passengers. These were to include two high-ranking Japanese officers, one an aircraft specialist, the other a submarine expert. The rest of the VIP party included a German Air Force general with staff, and a Navy judge advocate, Commander A. Nieschling, himself on a special mission.[2]

The most top-secret item of the cargo was the reported shipment of fissionable uranium-235. It was carefully crated in wooden boxes and in special charge of the Japanese officers, Colonel M. Shoshi, an aircraft construction engineer, and Engineer Commander Hideo Tomanaga, the submarine specialist. Because of the coincident similarity of the German Navy abbreviation for submarines, U-boat, and the symbol U, denoting the metallic element uranium, the significance of the lethal cargo was missed, even after its accidental discovery by the ship's radio officer, Chief Petty Officer Wolfgang Hirschfeld. The crates, measuring twenty-five centimeters square, were wrapped in heavy brown paper and sealed. They bore an inscription in Japanese script and the symbol U-235.

When asked to declare the contents of the crates, one of the Japanese officers stated that it was "cargo from the U-235 which is not now sailing to Japan." When Hirschfeld made a routine check with Fleet Headquarters he was told that submarine U-235 (Type VII C) had never been, and was not now, earmarked to sail to Japan. In the rush of getting ready for the voyage, and in the face of increasingly alarming war news—that the U.S. Army had crossed the Rhine, that the Soviets were closing in on Berlin—nothing more was done about the crates at the time. They remained stowed below deck close to the cots allotted to the Japanese officers. As part of their extensive diplomatic baggage, the contents of the crates were never probed. And Captain Fehler made no reference to it.[3]

The possibility that the crates did in fact contain uranium-235 is not discounted by experts. Unknown to Allied scientists, the Germans had been able to build up a sizeable stockpile of U-235 and had held up to two tons, as well as two tons of heavy water. In 1945, a senior German nuclear scientist pretended that the entire stockpile was no greater than a walnut-sized piece of uranium. Japan's own nuclear development paralleled that of Germany's slow progress, which sagged around 1942, when the U.S. A-bomb effort was getting underway. To the chagrin of U.S. nuclear scientists, Japan's cyclotrones were destroyed by unbriefed invading American troops. Almost to the end of the war in Europe, the United States believed that the German atomic work was dangerously close to the U.S. program, which climaxed with the dropping of two atom bombs on Japan on August 6 and 9, 1945, on Hiroshima and Nagasaki.[4]

In April 1945, less than four months before the A-bombs were dropped, Tokyo was not even blacked out. Night life on the Ginza was in full swing, and the crew of the *U-234*, just emerging from a long, drab fitting-out period in war-economy-geared, blacked-out Germany, was much looking forward to a stint in prewar luxury. In addition to a Japanese ensign, earmarked to be displayed as a courtesy flag upon entering Japanese territorial waters, the sub also carried invitation cards in Japanese for the reception the officers and crew had planned on arrival.

Because of damage en route to Norway, *U-234* did not sail until April 16, when it finally left Europe. At sea, it totally missed the Allied cease-fire order on May 5 and was well into the Atlantic on May 8, the day a monitored newscast brought news of the unconditional surrender of all German forces. It was a doubly black day for all aboard *U-234* when they heard that the two Japanese officers had taken their own lives rather than face being taken as prisoners of war by the enemy. Japan was still at war with the United States and Britain.

Their deaths had profoundly affected Fehler, as he recently told me in Hamburg. By the time the double suicide was discovered, both officers were beyond revival, Fehler recalled. Beside their cot was a telltale empty bottle of Luminal (phenobarbitone).

A farewell message in English pinned to one of the pillows read:

> Dear Captain:
> We are not permitted to fall into enemy hands alive. In case we should still be alive when you find us, please leave us alone and let us die.[5]

On May 13 *U-234* first broke wireless silence since leaving Norway. The signal was picked up by a Canadian warship off the Canadian coast, in British territorial waters. For the next five days Fehler played tag with the Canadians, flashing false coordinates of his position. It was just a ruse to give him time to leave British waters—he preferred being taken prisoner by the U.S. Navy.

The ruse worked. Once inside U.S. territorial waters, Fehler made contact with the U.S. Navy and was ordered to stand by to surrender to the U.S. Navy escort destroyer *Sutton*, based on nearby Portsmouth, New Hampshire. Fehler did not plan that the crew of the *Sutton* would get a chance to lay hands on the Japanese officers, even in death. But because of bad weather, their burial at sea could not be arranged. Then shortly before the *U-234* was due to be boarded by an American prize crew, Fehler prepared the burial ceremony.

The bodies of the dead officers, wrapped in their hammocks, were brought up on deck. The Japanese ensign was then wrapped around Colonel Shoshi's body. By way of a last gesture, Captain Fehler fetched the samurai sword Commander Tomonaga had entrusted to him for safekeeping before they set sail. Kneeling on the deck, Fehler secured it to Tomonaga's body. The two bodies were slipped overboard. The burial ceremony was conducted according to Christian rites, and after it was over, with them went their diplomatic baggage, the heavy small crates said to have contained uranium-235, and several heavy metal cylinders believed by Fehler to contain documents.

After its boarding by the American prize crew, the *U-234* put in at Portsmouth harbor on May 19, 1945. At the end of July news got around that the German submarine had reportedly carried a cargo of uranium. The vessel was immediately checked over with Geiger counters. According to a member of the *U-234* mission, the local Portsmouth paper carried an item that day stating that, had there been a nuclear explosion aboard the sub, it would have wiped out "half of Portsmouth."

KAMMLER'S NEXT MOVE

The field of conspiracy is like the
Sargasso.
PROFESSOR ARTHUR CECIL PIGOU

O F THE LAY OBERAMMERGAU Passion Players who
staged the dramatization of the Crucifixion of Christ every
ten years, only Hans Zwinck, who played the treacherous
Judas, had nothing to fear from the approaching Americans. He was the only non-Nazi member of the cast. Two
years after the war, in 1947, a local deNazification prosecutor described Zwinck as the "only OK German in the
village." Even Alois Lang, portrayer of Christ in the two
productions before 1945, was a Nazi party member.

In early April 1945, the stocky, gray-bearded owner of the
biblical-frescoed Haus Jesu Christi Hotel, today known as
the Alois Lang Hotel, was busy providing whatever com-
forts and extra services he was able to rustle up for the VIP
occupant of the best suite of the hotel. His guest was the
legendary favorite of both Himmler and Hitler, SS General
Kammler, who had just arrived.

There was no sign of war in the cluster of picturesque
villages that spread out as far above the valley as one could
see. It was very close to the Austrian border. Kammler's
sudden presence at the tourist and winter sports center was
unscheduled. It came about on orders of the German Gen-

eral Staff, when it realized that the Reich's last punch, its main V-2 rocket production center, with all its secrets, was unexpectedly within the reach of both the United States and the Red Army, rolling in from the east along the northern coast of the Pomeranian Bay.

This had been the second forced evacuation of the Peenemunde rocket group and its data and blueprints within three action-packed months. The first move was prompted by the Red Army's rapid advance, in the face of tough SS resistance, to within a close proximity of Usedom Peninsula, where Peenemunde was located. Somehow Peenemunde had escaped serious bombardment over the years, until this near-fatal blow was administered in August 1943. The raid was so unexpected that it completely surprised Wernher von Braun and his VIP guest, Flight Captain Hanna Reitsch. She was the daredevil aviatrix who had flight-tested the flying bomb (V-1) forerunner of the United States and Soviet Cruise missiles of the 1980s. They had no inkling a raid was in the offing and only narrowly escaped with their lives.

By April 6, 1945, the spearhead of the United States Third Division's Combat Command B, under Brigadier General Truman E. Boudinot, had reached the approaches to the well-concealed Nordhausen underground aircraft plant and nearby Bleicherode, where the technical staff made its headquarters. But by then the coveted "bird had flown its coop" and was well beyond the first leg of its 500-mile trip to Oberammergau.

The interminably long train of evacuees from Nordhausen—mostly sleepers and well-stocked diners—was escorted by a strong detachment of Kammler's SS troops, drawn from his command of the Nordhausen area. Many were recruited from the disbanded V-1 and V-2 Reprisal Corps, which under Kammler had run the offensive against

London and other civilian targets in Britain and the Continent in 1944.

In a rare exhibition of German black humor, the train was nicknamed the *Vergeltungs Express* ("Reprisal Express"), though everyone on the rocket chessboard had realized that the time had passed to talk of retaliation. It was an open secret that the group had expected to surrender to the United States Army within the foreseeable future. There was no realistic alternative in the offing. The group arrived in Oberammergau on April 7. Chief designer Wernher von Braun, his arm in a plaster cast after a car accident, and Dornberger, Kammler's deputy, made their way separately.

The Peenemunde rocket project was so secret that when an experimental V-2 crashed and almost totally destroyed a nearby Luftwaffe base, news of the catastrophe was covered up. Subsequently plans were made to test the rockets elsewhere. The range was at Blizna, Poland, near Warsaw.

Neither the RAF nor the British scientists under Dr. R.V. Jones, the original recipient of the 1939 *Oslo Report*, had any idea of the German plans to build what turned out to be the world's first long-range rocket missile.

The first tip-off that the Germans were actually engaged and well ahead with a super-secret rocket project came late in 1942. It keynoted a British intelligence transcript of a bugged conservation between captured Afrika Korps Commander General Wilhelm Ritter von Thoma and another general, at a British prisoner-of-war camp in England. Speaking in undertones, and not suspecting a planted microphone, the two generals were overheard making reference to "the secret rocket project" Hitler had promised military leaders the previous year as the answer to Allied air superiority. It was due to be operational by the spring of 1945 and the project "was already eight months overdue."

Kammler's job was to ensure that the group had every facility to implement its original mandate to create an "ultimate weapon." The new weapon was to be a successor to the cannon and the bomber, as the new sophisticated multifaceted capabilities of the rocket missiles have gradually replaced the role of the manned long-range bomber. The high-priority switch to purely military projects at Peenemunde never dimmed the rocket group's deep-seated dedication to conquer space and interplanetary travel.

On March 7, 1945, when the U.S. Ninth Armored Division surprised even the Allied Supreme Command by unexpectedly crossing the Rhine at Remagen near Bonn, the first Allied formation to have done so, Kammler realized that the Reich's eventual military defeat in the field was only a matter of time. Soon the Allied forces under Supreme Commander U.S. General Dwight D. Eisenhower and the Red Army under Soviet Marshal Grigori Zhukov were headed for an early linkup. Kammler had been monitoring the narrowing gap very closely, ever since March.

The pending linkup was also very much in the minds of Eisenhower and Hitler. Both had regularly scanned the marked-up battle maps in their headquarters, pinpointing the day-by-day, hour-to-hour movements of the two vast armies. Apart from their obvious opposing interests, they were both mindful of the possibility that the linkup might flare into a bloody clash, as had occurred when German troops first came into contact with their former allies, the Soviets, before Hitler invaded Russia in 1941. But, while Eisenhower hoped that it would not happen, Hitler, in a classic display of malicious joy, obviously looked forward to it.

Kammler's thoughts at the moment were more occupied with the increasing likelihood that Nordhausen would be overrun and would provide its captors with a bonanza of hundreds of completed V-1s and V-2s, as well as jet engines for the ME-262. It was a tossup whether the Red Army, in whose designated zone Nordhausen would fall on the ending of hostilities, or the U.S. Third Army would get there first.

Over breakfast at Oberammergau, Kammler reviewed the situation calmly. Under the circumstances, he did not fancy the prospect of being in such close proximity with the scientists. He was very much aware that he was intensely disliked both by Dornberger and von Braun. Kammler had always made it clear that he distrusted both. And the feeling was mutual. For one thing, on arrival at Oberammergau, the group failed to understand why Kammler, though technically in command, should be in Oberammergau instead of acting under his new authority as Reich plenipotentiary for all modern aircraft production. By rights he should be touring aircraft factories to expedite production of the ME-262.

The document spelling out Kammler's new authority represented the most important promotion of his career. It also capped Himmler's ambition to put the SS into a policy-making operational slot in the aircraft industry. The letter of appointment, issued in the Reich Chancellory bunker, carried the solid black rubber stamp overprint GEHEIME KOMMANDOSACHE ("Top Secret Command Matter"). It provided the first official documentation of Hitler's complete distrust of both Goering and Speer, by subordinating both to Kammler in all matters of modern aircraft production.

The sweeping authority Hitler conferred on Kammler was unprecedented on a further score. To rub in the fact that they had been superseded, Hitler made both Goering and Speer countersign the letter of appointment. (It is not known whether Kammler was superstitious and attached any significance to the fact that his copy of the document, executed in seventeen copies, happened to bear the number 13.) On paper Kammler's latest bailiwick still covered considerable territory. In April the shrinking Reich, eroding in the east, west, and south, still controlled Norway, Denmark, northern Germany around Hamburg, southern Bavaria around Munich, Czechoslovakia, Austria, and a slice of Italy, including the port of Genoa.

Pending Dornberger's arrival, von Braun, acting head of the group of scientists at Oberammergau, was bothered by two problems. First, at the final collapse, the fanatical SS guards might destroy everything of potential value to the Americans, and second, perhaps some might even attempt to decimate the group of scientists. He was aware of Kammler's orders to the SS rear guard that he left at Nordhausen, to defend it to the last, but if they failed, to blow it up in accordance with the wishes of the Supreme Command. It was taken for granted that the surviving slave laborers should not be left to tell the tale.

After consultations with members of the group, von Braun found consensus on two major points. First, Kammler's chances for acting on his new instructions in developing, testing, and producing improved versions of the ME-262, even expediting its production, had virtually sunk to zero over the past fortnight. Second, the High Command's orders for the resumption of research at Oberammergau were unfulfillable. The only logical explanation the group had for Kammler's presence was the growing conviction that he might be planning to use the group as hostage in negotiations with the Americans, should he still be around. Some members of the group discounted the possibility that Kammler would ever get the chance to negotiate. As an SS general and with his known record, it was unlikely that the Americans would recognize his command after a surrender. They assumed that the group and Kammler would be separated at once.

The experts were further aware of the key fact that any negotiations likely to take place would stand or fall with the physical possession of the documents. Without them V-2s could neither be manufactured nor developed, short of starting from scratch with experts having the necessary know-how.

Von Braun reassured the group that Kammler never had access to the documents and had no idea of their present whereabouts. The generally accepted story is that von Braun, in a preemptive move, had all documents, blueprints, drawings, research data, and wind tunnel tests—the essence of V-2 research and development since 1932—buried in the gunpowder chamber of a disused coal mine. Only two trusted engineers who picked the site had any idea of their location. The hiding place was at Dörnten, between Goslar and Salzgitter, near Nordhausen.

Neither von Braun nor Dornberger was aware that Kammler, for several years past, had access to far more advanced projects, including the missile field at the SS research think tank at Pilsen. The group concluded that the most likely explanation for Kammler's continued presence in the area was Oberammergau's easy access to a number of major aircraft manufacturing centers, the doors of which would automatically be open to him. As government subcontractors, all plans came under his new authority.[1]

The wide abundance of high-technology military hardware and supporting blueprints in the area would have made any international arms dealer's mouth water. A nearby Messerschmitt plant, camouflaged to resemble a Bavarian inn, still turned out turbojet engines and other components for the ME-262, which easily outpaced all Allied fighters operational at the time. Bayrische Motorenwerke BMW, another airforce subcontractor with a store of secret data and blueprints on past, current, and future projects, was also operational. The super-modern, for those days, Mach-4 wind tunnel at nearby Kochelsee, run under cover of hydroelectric waterworks, was also in full swing. It had replaced the Peenemunde wind tunnel destroyed by the RAF on August 17, 1943. Plans to boost the capacity of the wind tunnel to a record speed of 6,250 mph had been completed, providing invaluable aerodynamic data for high-speed, supersonic performance at high altitudes.[2]

Von Braun and his group were aware that the Messerschmitt and BMW archives also contained valuable data on recently abandoned—but under normal conditions, potentially viable—projects that could be brought to fruition by any nation with the requisite funds, experts, and facilities. Kammler, though also well aware of this potential, had cancelled some of the projects in February 1945, as part of a streamlining operation. The shelved projects included:

1. Work on various versions of air-to-air, air-to-ground, and similar homing rockets, forerunners of the German-designed, French-coproduced Exocet series of the 1980s.

2. The experimental, forward-swept-wing JU-287 fighters, able to land and take off at slow speeds from short runways, a principle incorporated in various modern aircraft designs.

3. A reusable forty-ton glider, envisaged at the time to fly ammunition to German troops on the eastern front in Russia and to evacuate the wounded. The glider was also to be used in the projected invasion of Britain. A test flight of an experimentally engined prototype was shown in *Deutsche Wochenschau*, an official newsreel to boost home morale. It was screened against the musical backdrop of Wagner's "Ride of the Valkyries" with the intention that the image of the nine spear-wielding, helmeted goddesses of Nibelung fame would suggest that victory was on its way. Nevetherless, the symbolic suggestion of victory overlooked the story line of the opera, that the actual mission of the warrior maiden was to carry home to Valhalla (the hall of the gods) the bodies of heroes slain in battle.

4. A truly war-economy-minded coapplication of obsolete fighters and bombers such as the veteran Junkers JU-88 twin-engine bomber and a Focke-Wulf 190 fighter. The bomber was to be used as a one-way bomb, carrying 4,000 tons of explosives, no crew, no armor-plating, no radar. It would be set off close to the target on a pre-aimed short course by the pilot of the Focke-Wulf 190 riding piggyback atop the bomber.[3]

In the course of one of the interviews the author had with Voss in 1949, which covered Skoda's role in the Reich's wartime arms program, he also discussed the general complex of shelved projects, their potential to a power that came into possession of relevant documentation, and the international patents situation, pending restoration of German sovereignty. Voss was very frank—any very senior German official with the necessary authority would have had no difficulty in sequestering any blueprint or document he wanted.[4] His views were echoed by a retired Skoda executive formerly attached to the Skoda main office in Prague. In the view of this executive, a cache of blueprints so acquired would have been worth its weight in gold to the ultimate recipient, in saved research and development costs alone.

In spite of his spectacular successes, Kammler had always managed to steer clear of open clashes and turned a blind eye to the envy and jealousy he aroused in others. Whenever he felt that a bit of diplomacy would suit his purpose Kammler spread it on thick, especially with Dornberger and von Braun, both of whom he needed. Kammler was aware of the latter's lack of popularity with his fellow scientists, so he took particular care to treat him with courtesy.

Von Braun, of course, never trusted Kammler, whose rapid

rise to the top stood in sharp contrast with his own and Speer's eclipse in the charmed circle of Hitler's ever-decreasing circle of favorites. That week in Oberammergau early in 1945, von Braun rolled back his memory to the first time he and Kammler met. Bad blood between them had began early in 1944, when it became obvious that the V-2 would become a spectacular weapon. This prompted Himmler to make his first major bid to get on the V-2 bandwagon, with a bid for the operation. The attempt was blocked by Dornberger, but the SS kept on trying. In March 1944, Himmler asked von Braun to join the SS. When he refused, Himmler had him arrested, accusing him of putting higher priority on space exploration than on essential military projects. It took a joint effort by Speer and Dornberger to get von Braun released. Speer assured Hitler that, without von Braun, "there would be no V-2s." The man Himmler had earmarked for the V-2 operation was Kammler. In due course, Himmler had his way.

After the abortive July 20 uprising against Hitler in 1944, the SS emerged as the most trusted Reich body. Kammler cashed in on this. With Hitler's backing he took over all V-2 construction at Peenemunde and was promoted from brigadier general to lieutenant general. With that promotion, Dornberger became the number-two man. He never forgave Kammler, von Braun recalled in Oberammergau.[5] Another clash with Kammler had come in January 1946, as the rapid advances of the Red Army on Peenemunde prompted von Braun to urge Kammler to evacuate the site to Nordhausen or the second alternate site at Ebensee, Traunsee, in Austria's Salzkammergut region, where Kammler had also built an underground production facility. Kammler absolutely refused to consider the possibility of evacuation, until the move to Nordhausen became inevitable. Kammler's subsequent insistence on having a batch of incompletely tested V-2s shipped to the Western front, despite von Braun's advice to the contrary, had failed to improve the atmosphere.

For approximately one week that early April 1945, Kammler did not contact the Peenemunde group. Finally he asked von Braun to see him. In the absence of Dornberger, von Braun was still in charge of the group. The meeting took place at the Haus Jesu Christi Hotel, where Kammler and his adjutant *SS Obersturmbannführer* Starck had made their headquarters.

While waiting to see Kammler, von Braun, filling in time in a room adjoining Kammler's suite, overheard a conversation between Kammler and his adjutant. Recalling the occasion to a U.S. intelligence officer[6] after his surrender, von Braun described the gist of the conversation he overheard. He said he was astounded to hear that the two were discussing the possibility of eluding American capture by taking refuge at the nearby fourteenth-century Ettal Abbey and assuming the garb of the Benedictine order, famous for the Chartreuse-type Ettal liqueur made by the monks. Starck proposed that Kammler should burn his SS uniform, whereupon Kammler said, who knew, he might even find a new postwar career as a liqueur salesman.

Hearing footsteps, von Braun moved away from the door. Colonel Starck then asked him to step inside. Von Braun told his interrogator that throughout the meeting that followed with Kammler, Starck had kept his machine pistol within reach. Kammler, cool, inquired whether the Peenemunde group was comfortable and whether it would be possible to resume research.

Von Braun answered in the affirmative to both, concealing the fact that the group had written off the chances of resuming research in earnest. Von Braun then requested permission to disperse the group to neighboring villages, to present "less of a target" than in the uncamouflaged SS barracks they were occupying, and Kammler readily agreed. Kammler finally informed von Braun that he would be leaving Oberammergau "for an indefinite period" and said good-bye.

He did not feel it necessary to inform von Braun that he had seen Hitler on April 3, that he had conferred with him at length, discussing the reorganization of the Luftwaffe, which Hitler had put in his hands. Kammler's meeting with Hitler at the *Führerbunker* is reported at some length in Propaganda Minister Josef Goebbels's diary[7] entry of April 4, recording the events of April 3. "The Führer had a very long meeting with SS Obergruppenführer Kammler who now shoulders the major responsibility for implementing the Luftwaffe reform." Goebbels was impressed with Kammler's apparently indomitable spirit. He wrote admiringly that Kammler was behaving "in a splendid fashion" and that Hitler "pinned great hopes on him."

In a related entry, covering events of March 31, Goebbels recalled the sweeping authority Hitler had conferred on Kammler on March 27, when he had put Kammler in charge of the Messerschmitt 262 jet fighter production, which Hitler regarded as vital for the Reich's survival.

> The Führer has now conferred extraordinarily wide authority on SS Obergruppenführer Kammler. At the moment the Führer wants to restrict the Luftwaffe reform to a very limited program, but he wants an all-out effort to put it through. It must be implemented at all cost. Goering feels that the new authority conferred on Kammler had very definitely pushed him (Goering) in the corner, but there is just nothing he can do about it.

During the meeting with von Braun at Oberammergau, Kammler purposely covered up the fact that while in Berlin to confer with Hitler, he had also had a meeting with Speer. There was no love lost between Kammler and Speer either. Aware that Kammler was being groomed both by Hitler and Himmler to replace him in the Cabinet at the first opportunity, Speer's hatred for Kammler, whose professional skills he admired, was deep-seated. It had been building up over the years, as Kammler began to eclipse both Speer and Goering in Hitler's favor. Speer was especially envious of Kammler's appointment as plenipotentiary for the construction of the ME-262. The appointment, Speer had to concede, put an end to his and Goering's ambitions for the control of the aircraft industry. The two had been engaged in bitter struggle and intrigue over it for several years.

According to Speer, writing almost forty years later, Kammler squarely suggested during their meeting on April 3 that he should leave Berlin and join him in Munich, that the war was lost, and that Speer would have a better chance if he made the move now.[8] Speer did not take up the suggestion. He recalled that during the meeting, his last ever with Kammler, the general no longer exhibited his usual "smart and dashing" attitude, that he had appeared unsure of himself and uneasy. In the course of the meeting Kammler had claimed that there were "moves afoot" to remove the führer. If they were successful, Kammler planned to contact the Western Allies and offer them the turbojet, missile, and other very high-technology research secrets in return for his personal freedom. He had already made plans to summon all relevant experts to Upper Bavaria to prepare the proposed deal, he told Speer.

Speer recalled in his book that, at war's end, rumors had circulated in Germany and France that Kammler had already made contact with the Allies[9] in November 1944. Being very close to Himmler, Kammler was most likely to have been aware, at the time of his meeting with Speer, that Himmler's secret negotiations for a surrender with the Allies had reached the first contact stage.

*　　*　　*

Kammler's subsequent actions appear to be in direct contradiction with the picture Speer had painted of him as of April 3. He had made no attempt to maintain contact with the Peenemunde group. This would have been essential if he were to lay the groundwork for negotiations with the Allies.

Captured records show that in Kammler's last weeks in power, he was working away from his Berlin headquarters. During this time, in sharp contrast to the legendary drive Speer and others had associated with him, Kammler went about implementing his sweeping authority in an inexplicably superficial fashion, the like of which he would never have tolerated from subordinates. In one flagrant example of the indifference he was now showing in contrast to the strictest professionalism and personal touch that had always armed his work, he reportedly assigned a lowly *SS Obersturmbannführer* ("lieutenant") to run the job of expediting ME-262 production.

There was also growing evidence that Kammler had no intention of returning to the corridors of power in Berlin. He had largely given first hint of this to Speer on April 3, suggesting that the minister should join him in Munich. Speer later recalled that Kammler preferred to be as far away from Hitler as possible should "things go wrong."

In Munich, Kammler worked out of the regional branch of the Waffen SS and Reich Police Construction Office, an offshoot of his construction empire, instead of calling in the staff and facilities of the air and armaments ministries, as was his right under his March 27 appointment. Thus, instead of using experts, familiar with the bottleneck in jet aircraft production, he relied on civil engineers.

By mid-April, Kammler no longer concealed his intention of staying away from the Berlin scene. He boldly appointed his own plenipotentiary for speeding the production of the superfast ME-262 jet, and assigned him to the

Armaments and War Production Ministry. The man he picked was V-2 production expert Gerhard Degenkolb. The new switch confused matters even more and completely distorted the established chain of command. Suddenly there were two plenipotentiaries for the ME-262 production. Kammler himself, by virtue of the authority vested in him by Hitler, which officially subordinated both Speer and Goering to the execution of this assignment, and Degenkolb, under personal assignment from Kammler. Under the circumstances, Speer and Otto Karl Saur, head of the Office for Armaments and Munition at the Speer Ministry, had no alternative but to approve the Degenkolb appointment.

Because of the chain of events, Kammler's last recorded official communication, a service message to Himmler on April 17, deserves more than a cursory examination. Marked SECRET, the four-line message, routed to the office of the Reich Leader SS, seems a far cry from the type of classified communication a senior Waffen SS general, regarded as the most powerful man in Germany outside the Cabinet, would be expected to send his Commander in Chief, one of the most important Germans in the Cabinet. The communication sounds more like the type of signal a junior officer would send his commanding officer to assure him that he was busy and on the ball.

The message Kammler chose to classify secret and transmit at that critical juncture was to put on record that a truck, earmarked for handing over to the Junkers aircraft factory, could not be released from Kammler's motor pool, as it was needed for his operation. Mark the fact that the reference was to one truck as distinct from a motor pool of trucks. The rest of the message is a routine assurance that "work on expediting jet aircraft production is progressing in accordance with the Führer's orders." That was all there was to the message.

Assuming that the signal was genuine, that it was not engineered as a coverup for Kammler's presence elsewhere, the format of the message and procedure used appear to suggest that Kammler was physically present at the office where the message had originated on April 17, and that he had personally signed or initialed the text before its transmittal. The authenticity or nonauthenticity of the message, in that it pinpoints Kammler as being in Munich on April 17, is relevant, since it was the last ever recorded communication from him, before the *Götterdämmerung* or since.

For the record and for readers with a penchant for detective work, it should be noted that under German communications procedure, the letters "Gez" preceding the originator's name are intended to note that the person whose name appears as the sender had signed the message before it was transmitted. "Gez" stands for *Gezeichnet*, "signed by." A message sent on behalf of the sender would show the letters "I.A."—*Im Auftrag*, "by order of," indicating that the originator was not physically present.

Meanwhile the last phase of the war was unfolding rapidly. On April 21, U.S. and Red Army forces linked up at Torgau on the Elbe River, southeast of Berlin. On April 22, the first Russian shells dropped in the Berlin Reich Chancellory gardens. On April 24, behind Hitler's back, Himmler opened negotiations with the Western Allies, offering unconditional surrender in the west but continuation of the war in the east. The offer was flatly rejected on April 28.

The pincer of Russian armor was rapidly closing in on Berlin. Russian troops were fighting in the streets, and the rape of Berlin was on. The civilian inhabitants of the once formidable city were taking a terrible beating. As T.S. Eliot rightly remarked: "April is the cruelest month, breeding lilacs out of the dead land."

On the night of April 30, a Monday, nightingales were

singing along Berlin's Wannsee Lake when Hitler took his own life in the Chancellory bunker. He had gone underground on January 16. The news was withheld until the next day, May 1. Dornberger, who had made his personal headquarters at the skiing resort Oberjoch, above Oberammergau, heard the newsflash and made the last of his several abortive attempts to contact Kammler. He had been out of touch with the group for more than twenty-one days. As "Kammler was no longer around," Dornberger resumed his overall command of the Peenemunde group that day.

The same day, Grand Admiral Karl Doenitz, Hitler's designated successor as Commander in Chief and head of state, took office in Flensburg near the Danish border, in Northern Germany. On May 2, the day Berlin capitulated to the Red Army, Dornberger and his group surrendered to the U.S. 44th Infantry Division, just across the border, in Austria.

By May 7, the Peenemunde group was under lock and key at a U.S. 7th Army prisoner-of-war cage at Garmisch-Partenkirchen. The ensuing tug of war with U.S. authorities in Washington over terms and conditions of the service contract that the core of the Peenemunde group was in the process of negotiating for employment as rocket specialists in the United States was completed on May 21. It was sealed by the handing over of the Peenemunde research documents to the U.S. Army.[10]

The documents, weighing some fourteen tons, had been retrieved from the cache where von Braun had them buried to keep them from falling into the hands of the Red Army. The crated documents were en route to the United States only hours before their hiding place became part of the British zone of Germany. It was just in the nick of time. Otherwise Britain would have bagged the research secrets, and perhaps the first man on the moon would have been a Briton!

Kammler's name dramatically leaped into the limelight

some six weeks after he had last contacted the rocket group, and five weeks after his last recorded communication from Munich. It was May 21, thirteen days after the German surrender, the very day von Braun and his group received the green light on their U.S. contracts. It came during Speer's last interrogation prior to his arrest, by members of the U.S. Strategic Bombing Survey Mission at Glückstadt, close to the seat of the Doenitz government, of which Speer was a member. When a member of the mission[11] questioned Speer on the operational use of the V-2 and asked for technical details, Speer found himself out of his depth. So he told the mission: *"Ask Kammler, he has all the facts and figures."*

On May 21, then, Speer assumed that Kammler was contactable and could be sent for, should the mission require his testimony in regard to one of the major unclarified aspects of the war. Speer's reaction is relevant to the Kammler story from now on. It was also significant that the panel did not ask Speer to identify Kammler.

It must be assumed that the mission was fully well aware who Kammler was. It knew that it was he who built and ran the underground aircraft and missile factory at Nordhausen, with its bonanza of complete V-2s and jet engines that had fallen into U.S. hands in April. It also knew that the cream of its stockpile of missiles was in the process, even as the Speer interrogation was in progress, of being crated for immediate shipment to the United States. Kammler's very close relations with Hitler and Himmler must also have been known.

Under the circumstances, the mission was in a position to put an immediate tracer on Kammler's whereabouts through the American Prisoner of War Information Unit (APWI) in Munich, the area where Kammler was last heard of. In view of his prominent rank and his status as an "automatic arrestee," the APWI would have been able to establish whether Kammler was being held, whether he was still at large, or in British or French custody. The information should have been of urgent interest to the American mission and most certainly of personal interest to Speer.[12] No record exists that such a checkup was made.

The exchange between Speer and the U.S. mission with the reference to Kammler appears in a microfilm copy of the original interrogation transcripts, corrected in Speer's own hand. The document was made available to me by the U.S. National Archives. An earlier request to the British Public Record Office for the release of the Speer interrogation reports, known to be on file in London because of their extensive remarks involving Britain, was turned down on the grounds that the papers are scheduled to remain closed indefinitely, possibly until the year 2020. Instead of the usual thirty-year rule, Britain appears to be considering applying the rare seventy-five-year rule.

In my belief, the continued closure of the reports was prompted by Speer's very critical assessment of RAF bombing strategy and his allegations that the RAF Bomber Command preferred to bomb cities rather than industrial targets. The transcript also carried Speer's veiled suggestion that the Western Allies had tacitly helped Germany in staving off a Soviet swoop to the Rhine. Speer had also expressed surprise at what he termed the "surprisingly low morale" of the British civilian population at the height of the V-weapons offensive.

There has been no confirmed news or sighting of Kammler since April 17, 1945. This is one of a series of bizarre interlocking facts that has prompted the author to follow Kammler's trail over the years, on the off chance that it might provide a clue to the loss to the Soviets of the SS research think-tank nest egg of Nazi research secrets on May 12, 1945, at the Skoda Works in Pilsen, Czechoslovakia.

UNEXPECTED PRIZE

Not infrequently, what later prove to
be the most significant events, take
place unrecognized as such, at the
time.

ANONYMOUS SEVENTEENTH-CENTURY
JURIST

UNBEATEN JAPAN, astride countless islands in the
vast archipelago it had conquered during the war, had not
slipped from the minds of American troops in Europe, as
they stood by for the imminent German surrender. U.S.
troops knew only too well that the Japanese war was still
a grim reality that lay ahead, and that they faced several
years of bloody island-hopping. The Japanese were, of course,
a very different race, and did not know the concept of surrender.

Thousands of American troops were already on their way
to the Pacific. The First U.S. Army Headquarters, the first
American contingent in Europe to be slated for redeploy-
ment to the Pacific, received its marching orders the very
day other American troops captured Hitler's birthplace,
Braunau. In the chaos that cocooned the German side,
countless people were uprooted, countless trails were lost,
countless serving German soldiers, sailors, and airmen were

awaiting to hear the effective date of the inevitable surrender. Kammler, no longer the most powerful man in Germany outside the Cabinet, had disappeared from the scene as of April 17.

Though official records that have come to light over the past several decades make no reference to Kammler nor pinpoint his movements after that date, other material that has surfaced in the course of following his trail suggests that he did not remain in the U.S. zone. He had taken a circuitous route to Czechoslovakia, then still under German control. To head east at such a time, when entire populations, like leaves caught in a whirlwind, were fleeing westward, seems more than strange. This is particularly true since Kammler well knew that, under the terms of Allied accords dating back several years, Czechoslovakia was to come under Soviet occupation at the end of hostilities and would most likely remain in the Soviet orbit. Accordingly, Allied planning, mindful of the arrangements, initially between the exiled Czechoslovak government and Moscow, did not plan on advancing beyond the Czechoslovak border.

At the end of April, Prague was still firmly held by German Field Marshal Ferdinand Schoerner's tough SS division. The Red Army was still bottled up east of Prague and was unable to take the capital until two days after the German surrender had come into effect. As far as Kammler was concerned, the Skoda Works at Pilsen continued to be in German hands and were likely to remain so until the Red Army broke through.

Pilsen, an easy forty miles inside Czechoslovakia, was the hub of the last remaining island of German resistance within a 400- by 150-mile territory still under German control. At the end of April, the Third Reich was reduced to an area of some 450 by 200 miles, bounded in the north by Dresden, reaching as far south as Zagreb, Yugoslavia, and including all of Czechoslovakia and large chunks of Austria.

As the Iron Curtain was about to be rung down across Europe, Kammler must have encountered an endless stream of panic-stricken families unwilling to live under the Soviets fleeing to the west. The refugees walked or hitched rides and made their way toward the U.S. and British zones of Germany as best as they could. The trekkers were part of a westward stream of an estimated 4 million German civilians from the eastern battlefields toward zones that might again become battlefields.

There is nothing unusual about the migration of civilians in war, but this was unique, as the westward trekkers were not retreating to a quiet, unscarred hinterland, but to bomb-torn central Germany. Beyond that lay a second military front, from which many of the same trekkers had previously been evacuated. There was a parallel, frantic scurrying of German and Quisling officials from the Protectorate.[1] The long-standing German policy of alternating between violent threats and honeyed promises was now a thing of the past.

There can be no telling what went on in Kammler's mind after the day he dropped out of sight. According to one of his wartime aides recently traced, Kammler would most likely have been accompanied by his Belgian Walloon driver, an *SS Hauptscharführer* ("sergeant"), seconded from one of the Francophone Walloon SS units serving with the Waffen SS. Kammler, who was fluent in French, and his driver were known to carry civilian clothing wherever they went. At that particular juncture, the source said, traveling in SS uniform would "not exactly have been healthy."[2]

Asked if he had any idea where Kammler might have been headed, the former aide shrugged his shoulders, then said with a grin: "One thing is *tot sicher* (dead certain). Having showered all those rockets all over England, he would want to steer clear of the British. He knew that he would most probably be put on trial for war crimes."

On May 2, the day after Hitler's suicide was announced, the U.S. Third Army was poised on the Czechoslovak border. The Red Army was still bogged down by SS troops east of Prague, with no immediate chance of breaking their hold before the surrender and moving on for a projected linkup with U.S. troops. Bradley decided that the situation called for a command decision and contacted Eisenhower for authority to cross into Czechoslovakia for a holding operation, pending the arrival of the Red Army.

Eisenhower reacted positively. On May 3 Bradley phoned Patton to give him the go-ahead. "Ike has just called. He said you have the green light for Czechoslovakia, George. When can you move?"

"Tomorrow morning," Patton said.[3]

It was typical for Patton, a nineteenth-century man and in every sense a Napoleonic-type general. He lived according to the tenets of his individualistic code of conduct. Bradley regarded him as "the ideal commander, with the drive and imagination for doing the dangerous things, fast." Patton knew he had Bradley's full confidence.

For the push into the German-run Slavic country, Patton was given the inexperienced 16th Armored Division, which was eager to get into combat before the war was over. With General Clarence R. Huebner's V Corps, Patton had just over half a million men under command, more than he ever had before.

His multipronged advance into Czechoslovakia was underway early on May 4. While one column uncovered evidence of German atrocities at the Mauthausen concentration camp near Linz, other Third Army columns soon crossed into Czechoslovakia. The target town was Pilsen, the home of the Skoda Works, the Reich's last operational armament production center.

For the GIs, some of whom had fought their way across Europe from Normandy, entering Czechoslovakia was at first an anticlimax. U.S. military historian Charles B. MacDonald recorded the event as it happened:

> The fighting was unusual, a comic opera war carried on by men who wanted to surrender, but seemingly had to fire a shot or two in the process. The land too was strange, neither German nor Czech.
>
> The little towns near the border, with their houses linked by fences and their decorated arches over the gates, had the look of Slavic villages, but the population was unquestionably hostile.
>
> This country was the disputed—mostly German in-habited—Sudetenland.
>
> The U.S. Armor was on the highway leading to the target town of Pilsen. Past silent undefended forts of Czechoslovakia, its undefended western fortifications, the "Little Maginot Line," the troops suddenly burst from the Sudetenland, with its apathetic, sometimes sullen German sympathizers, into a riotous land of colorful flags and cheering citizenry.
>
> As if they had stopped across some unseen barrier, the men found themselves in a new land of frenzy and de-light. It was Paris all over again, on a lesser scale and with different flags, but with the same jubilant faces, the same delirium of liberation.
>
> Past abandoned anti-aircraft guns that had protected the big Skoda industrial complex on the outskirts of the city, the armor raced into Pilsen.
>
> "*Nazdar! Nazdar!* Hello, Welcome," the people shouted.[4]

Pilsen and the Skoda Works were captured by Combat Command B. Third Armored Division, the same unit that captured Kammler's unique metropolis, with its treasure trove of missiles and jet engines, at Nordhausen in Saxony on April 11. CCB was no longer under the command of Brigadier General Truman E. Boudinot. After turning over command of Pilsen and the Skoda Works to another unit, CCB continued its eastward drive. No Red Army troops were in sight.

Patton, who never disguised his hate for the Russians, was determined to exploit the inability of the Red Army to make headway toward Prague and to capture it himself. Here was his chance. The way was wide open to win the Third Army the honor of liberating at least one European capital.

Eisenhower readily took the first step. He advised Moscow that, as the Red Army had no troops within 70 kilometers of the capital, he would advance toward Prague "if the situation required." Privately he suggested that Patton should drive on into Czechoslovakia, as the final boundaries, under which Czechoslovakia and the German provinces Thuringia and Saxony would be occupied by the Soviets after the end of hostilities, did not yet apply.

Unofficially, Patton's advance reconnaissance elements, on the move since dawn, had made the eighty-mile dash from the Czech border to Prague in record time and had already penetrated the outskirts of the capital the same day. They had flashed back the good news that the partisan command, with a great moral debt and strong ties to the Czechoslovak community in the United States, was ready to hand over Prague to the Americans before the Russians arrived.

Patton was elated with the news. Then the blow fell. He learned that Stalin had succeeded in bluffing Eisenhower into halting his eastward advance forty miles inside

Czechoslovakia. The hub of the easternmost limit was to be Pilsen. The boundary line stretched from the spa town Karlovy Vary (Karlsbad) in the north, to the brewery center Budejowicze (Budweis) south of Pilsen.

U.S. General John Dean, U.S. Military Mission chief in Moscow, had reported that Eisenhower's message, transmitted to General Alexei I. Antonov, chief of staff of the Red Army, had produced a "violent protest." Dean added: "Antonov's attitude showed the fine hand of the Soviet Foreign Office that Czechoslovakia was to be in the orbit of the Soviet Union, and that Czech gratitude to America for the liberation of its capital, was not part of the program."[5] Frustrated by the halt order, Patton asked Bradley if the Pilsen line was mandatory. What Patton had in mind was to drop out of contact for twenty-four hours, seize Prague, and report back from a telephone booth in Prague's historic Wenczeslas Square. Bradley had no choice but to come down on the plan.

The next day, on May 5, the Czech underground rose in revolt against the Germans and broadcast a desperate appeal for help to the Allies. On May 6, 1945, in a London dispatch from its staff correspondent John McCormick, *The New York Times* carried the following item. It was headed CZECH PATRIOTS TAKE PRAGUE.

> Dramatic calls for help were stemming from the Czech Radio this morning, indicating that the Germans were making an attempt to retake Prague from the force of Czech resistance. In a tone of extreme urgency the announcer said in English: "Calling all Allied armies. We need urgent help . . .Send your planes and tanks. Germans advancing on Prague. For the Lord's sake send help."

Bound by his agreement with Stalin, Eisenhower felt unable to respond to the dramatic appeal. The capital of

Czechoslovakia was left to the Soviets, as was Berlin, with all political advantages. On May 8, the day the war in Europe ended, Poland, over which Britain went to war, was in the grips of another dictator. The balance of power in Europe was just as dangerously distorted as it had been in 1940. On May 10, Prague joined the list of other European capitals already in Soviet hands: Berlin, Budapest, Vienna, Sofia, and Bucharest.

By early May the Soviet Union also held nearly one half of Germany and was to enlarge its hold when it moved into Saxony and Thuringia, which had been conquered by the United States with considerable loss of American lives. The *fait accompli* of Eisenhower's shortsighted decision had left Berlin beyond the reach of SHAEF correspondents. The Soviets refused to provide press facilities and the city was officially out of bounds, pending a green light from Moscow. When almost two months later U.S. and British military government teams were cleared by the Soviets to take over their sectors, they found that the Soviet sector included nearly one half of the city, including all key municipal offices, even the vaults of the Berlin banks.

Tantalizingly for correspondents accredited to SHAEF, all major newsbreaks regarding Hitler's death and the mysteries of the Chancellory bunker originated in Berlin, and there was no way to check them. All dispatches were based on the reports of the official Soviet news agency Tass. Western correspondents in Moscow could not file from Berlin and quoted Soviet sources. One wrote: "Russians find no trace of Hitler's body at the Chancellory Bunker." A likewise uncheckable London dispatch speculated that "the announcement of Hitler's death was only a clever hoax" and that the British "Foreign Office would demand production of Hitler's body after the hostilities." *The New York Herald Tribune,* on May 4, carried a dispatch quoting Hans Fritsche, chief of broadcasting at the Nazi Propaganda Ministry, that "Hitler's body had been hidden." Fritsche was then held by the U.S. 9th Army. From then on, news coverage of the final stages of the war became more and more subject to the strictures of the advancing Soviets, as city after city fell into their hands. News dispatches necessarily filed out of Paris or London, datelined SHAEF, filled the gap in most cases.

Six American correspondents, however, were determined that Berlin not remain a news-shadow area as far as the free world was concerned. Defying official Soviet *nyet*s and a SHAEF ban on coverage, pending Soviet clearance for a conducted and "supervised" tour, they made their own deal with a Red Army unit close to Berlin. On May 5, three days after the city had capitulated to the Red Army, the six enterprising newsmen wrote the first American eyewitness accounts of Berlin under Soviet rule.

One dispatch, by Ernest Leiser for *Stars and Stripes*[6], bannered BERLIN RUINS SYMBOLIZE COMPLETE NAZI DEFEAT, read:

> Berlin, the capital of defeat, today is the charred stinking broken skeleton of a city. It is impossible to believe that the disembowelled buildings, crater-pocked streets once could have been the capital of Greater Germany. . . .There are no shops, factories, office buildings for them to work in. . . .The Russian conquerors walk the streets with straggling prisoners. . . . cavalrymen wash their horses on the banks of the River Spree.

The proliferation of major news events that overwhelmed the SHAEF press corps that early May, including the impending coverage of two surrender ceremonies—one at Rheims, France, and the repeat ceremony in Berlin—inevitably had a side effect. Some stories that would normally have been staffed were relegated into a news-shadow area. It was on this score that the important event of the unexpected capture of the Skoda Works at Pilsen (May 6 by the U.S. Third Army, whose presence in Czechoslovakia had likewise not been expected) remained unstaffed. All dispatches reporting the capture were based on army briefings at SHAEF in Paris and London.

Even so, the event got top play, the last event to rate such prominent display before the German surrender story two days later. *The New York Times*, in a Paris dispatch from Drew Middleton on May 7, said, "Tanks and doughboys of General George S. Patton's Third Army, plunging deeper into Czechoslovakia, captured Pilsen, the site of the huge Skoda Armament center, the last left to the enemy." A five-column banner headline in *Stars and Stripes* read 3RD ARMY TANKS CAPTURE PILSEN.

The daily "American Press Summary," issued by the American Division of the British Ministry of Information in London, included in its summary of lead stories the capture of Pilsen.

PILSEN TAKEN

The Third Army, driving through heavy terrain, took Pilsen, the home of the Skoda Armament Works. The capture of Pilsen brings the U.S. Army to within 80 kilometers of Prague.

Banner headlines featured the taking of the Skoda Works and it was well known that it was the Reich's last remaining arms production center and of prime defense news interest. The feat of the six American correspondents who defied every obstacle to get into Berlin could not be matched in the case of Skoda's capture, and no newsmen were present.

My request of August 17, 1982 to the National Archives in Washington for the release of the relevant war diaries of the Third Army unit involved was sidetracked by the statement that "We were unable to locate any War Diaries" for the 16th Armored Division from May 6 to 12. It was not until 1949, four years after the capture of Skoda, that the cloud that settled on this news-shadow area, just as it slipped behind the Iron Curtain, was lifted. This occurred through a report brought to the author by the former German president of Skoda and the Hermann Goering Works, who witnessed the handover of the plant to the Red Army on May 12, 1945.

Dr. Wilhelm Voss (left) undergoing passport control at Rhine/Main Airport, Frankfurt on Main, accompanied by Col. Moaab, Adjutant of Egyptian Head of State General Muammed Naguib. *(dpa Bild, German Press Agency Photo, Frankfurt)*

Reich Protector of Bohemia and Moravia Baron Constantine von Neurath (in uniform at center) and Dr. Voss (on his right) on a tour of the Skoda plant in Pilsen in 1940.

Photo of Dr. Hans Kammler as it appears in his Nazi party record. *(Courtesy U.S. Document Center, Berlin)*

SS General Dr. Ing. Hans Kammler. *(Stern Magazine, Hamburg)*

(handwritten annotations at top)

Chef [d]er Führer

Brb.Nr. 4W /45 gKdos.Adj.F.

Führerhauptquartier,den 27.3.1945.

17 Ausfertigungen :
12.Ausfertigung.

Betr.: Strahlflugzeuge.

An

Verteiler.

Geheime Kommandosache

Der Einsatz von Strahlflugzeugen hat die absolute Überlegenheit über die feindlichen Maschinen erwiesen.

Es kommt jetzt darauf an, diesen Vorteil schnellstens durch Bereitstellung von genügenden Strahlflugzeugen zur Brechung des Luftterrors auszunutzen.

Dies kann nur durch Zusammenfassung aller verfügbaren Mittel des Reiches unter einer straffen Führung erfolgen.

Diese Aufgabe steht an Dringlichkeit vor allen anderen militärischen und wirtschaftlichen Maßnahmen.

Um dieses Ziel zu erreichen, erteile ich dem SS-Obergruppenführer und General der Waffen-SS Dr.Ing.Hans Kammler folgenden Auftrag :

1) Führung aller bis zum Einsatz erforderlichen Entwicklungen, Erprobungen und Fertigungen von Strahlflugzeugen und der zum Einsatz notwendigen Versorgungsmittel im Bereich des Reichsministers für Rüstung und Kriegsproduktion.

2) Führung aller bis zum Einsatz von Strahlflugzeugen erforderlichen Voraussetzungen im Bereich des Reichsministers der Luftfahrt und Oberbefehlshabers der Luftwaffe.

3) Die bisher auf dem Gebiete der Strahlflugzeuge im Bereich des Reichsministers für Rüstung und Kriegsproduktion erteilten Vollmachten gehen auf SS-Obergruppenführer und General der Waffen-SS Dr.Ing.Kammler über.

– 2 –

Der Generalbevollmächtigte des Oberbefehlshabers der Luftwaffe für Strahlflugzeuge wird ab sofort SS-Obergruppenführer und General der Waffen-SS Dr.Ing.Kammler unterstellt.

4) SS-Obergruppenführer und General der Waffen-SS Dr.Ing.Kammler ist mir für die Durchführung dieses Auftrages persönlich unterstellt und hat dazu alle Vollmachten. Er bedient sich hierzu sämtlicher Kommandodienststellen, Behörden und Einrichtungen der Wehrmacht, der Partei und des Reiches, die seinen Weisungen Folge zu leisten haben.

Der Führer
gez. Adolf Hitler

Der Reichsminister für
Rüstung und Kriegsproduktion
gez. Speer

Der Reichsmarschall
des Grossdeutschen Reiches
gez. Göring

Für die Richtigkeit :

Oberst,
Adjutant der Wehrmacht beim Führer.

Original   1.u.2.Ausf.
Verteiler:
Reichsmarschall   3.Ausf.
Reichsminister Speer   4.   "
Chef OKW   5.   "
Ob.d.M.   6.   "
Reichsführer-SS   7.   "
Chef der Reichskanzlei   8.   "
Leiter der Parteikanzlei   9.   "
Chef WFSt   10.   "
Chef Genst.Heer   11.   "
Chef Genst.Luftwaffe   12.   "
SS-Obergruppenführer und General
der Waffen-SS Kammler   13.   "
General d.Fl. Kammhuber   14.   "
Ministerialdirektor Dorsch   15.   "
Hauptdienstleiter Saur   16.   "
Adjtr.d.Wehrm.b.Führer   17.   "

Hitler's panic-motivated, last-minute Bunker Directive of March 27, 1945, appointing Kammler as chief of all modern aircraft production over the heads of Göring and Speer.

This *Who's Who in Nazi Germany* has been prepared for the use of those dealing with propaganda to and about Germany. It is CONFIDENTIAL. The information it contains may be used without restriction, but the source must not be disclosed.

The World War II British Intelligence *Who's Who in Nazi Germany* showing three references to Voss among leading Nazi personalities.

Dr. VOSS, Wilhelm
 Head of the Central Armaments Office in the Reich Ministry for Armaments and War Production, Director-General of the " Hermann Göring " Concern, Managing Director of the " Brünner Waffenwerke," President of the " Skoda " Works. (*Leiter des Zentralrüstungsamtes im Reichsministerium für Bewaffnung und Kriegsproduktion, Generaldirektor der "Reichswerke Hermann Göring," Generaldirektor der " Brünner Waffenwerke," Präsident der " Skoda-Werke "*). /Born in 1896, industrialist./

I. THE STATE

A. SUPREME REICH AUTHORITIES

REICH MINISTRIES

Armaments and War Production (" *Reichsministerium für Bewaffnung und Kriegsproduktion* ")
Reich Minister ... ... SPEER
Staatssekretär ... ... SCHULZE=FIELITZ
Heads of Divisions :—
 Ministerialdirektor ... ... SCHMEER
 Others ... DEGENKOLB - GEILENBERG - HETTLAGE - KEHRL - LIEBEL - PORSCHE - ROHLAND - SAUR - SCHAEDE - CLAHES - SCHIEBER - SEEBAUER - STOBBE=DETHLEFSEN - TIX - VOSS - WÄGER - WOLFF
Members of Armaments Council BÜCHER - FROMM - KESSLER - LEEB - MILCH - PLEIGER - PÖNSGEN - RÖCHLING - RÖHNERT - SPEER - THOMAS - VÖGLER - WÄGER - WITZELL (*a*) - ZANGEN
Under the Control of this Ministry :—
" Todt " Workers' Corps (" *Organisation Todt* ")
 Chief ... ... SPEER
 Front Command ... ... DORSCH

LEADING PERSONALITIES IN VARIOUS BRANCHES

MINING - METAL - MACHINE INDUSTRY :—

AVIENY	KALETSCH	RÖHNERT
BERVE	KNEPPER	ROHLAND
BRECHT	KOPPENBERG	SAUCKEL
BUSKÜHL	KRUPP	STEINBRINCK
CARP	LÖSER	TENGELMANN
FELLINGER	MESSER-	TGAHRT
FLICK	SCHMIDT	VIELMETTER
GOERENZ	MÜLLER	VÖGLER
HANIEL	PLEIGER	VOSS
HEINKEL	POENSGEN	WESSIG
HENSCHEL	PORSCHE	WILMOVSKY
HOUDREMONT	QUANDT	ZANGEN
JANASCHEK	RÖCHLING	

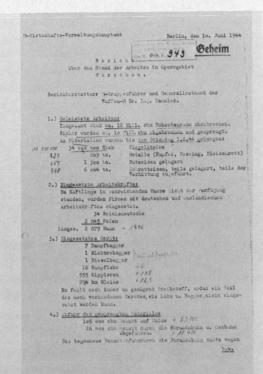

Kammler's report to Himmler, dated June 10, 1944, on the obliteration of the Warsaw ghetto, revealing that Kammler used 3,000 Polish workers under the supervision of 24 Reich Germans to annihilate the ghetto.

(top) Brigadier General Truman E. Boudinot, Commander of Combat Command B, 3rd Armored Division, Third Army who captured the underground aircraft and long range missile factory at Nordhausen (Harz) on April 11, 1945.

(middle) General Boudinot outside Gate 7 of Mittelwerke, Central Works, which made V-2 missiles and jet aero engines. *(Photos courtesy of Col. Truman E. Boudinot, Jr. and Lieut. Col. Burton E. Boudinot.)*

(bottom) Inmates of the DORA concentration and extermination camp, which supplied labor for Kammler's rocket factory.

Hermann A. Brassert, U.S. Engineering Executive, aboard the *Bremen* and his 1938 Christmas message to his close business associate Paul Pleiger, Board Chairman of the Hermann Göring heavy engineering complex with its unconventional signature "Heil Hitler!"

HERMANN A. BRASSERT

BERLIN-CHARLOTTENBURG 2
HARDENBERGSTRASSE 7

den 22. Dezember 1938.

Lieber Paul !

       Empfange zu Weihnachten und Neujahr meine besten Wünsche.

       Ich sende Dir hiermit als ein persönliches Weihnachtsgeschenk für Dich den Film über Corby und die Walzwerke der Inland Steel Company, die sicher von besonderem Interesse für Dich sind.

       Mit herzlichen Grüssen und

         Heil Hitler !

       Dein

       Hermann

Herrn Paul Pleiger,
BerlinW. 8,
Behrenstrasse 69a.

(Photo copyright Salzgitter AG, Archiv, Postfach, 3320 Salzgitter 41.)

The U-234, the last of the XB class 90 meter converted minelay-
ers, was launched by the Krupp-owned Germaniawerke in Kiel
on December 23, 1953, close to the fitting-out basin where the
world's first "Schnorkel" submarine breathing device (Walter) was
developed and tested.

STONEWALLING

A jewel, in a ten-times-barr'd up
chest.
SHAKESPEARE, *King Richard II*

Nᴇᴡs ᴛʜᴀᴛ Sᴋᴏᴅᴀ ʜᴀᴅ come under temporary
U.S. Army control on May 6 electrified the Western armament industry and the military. Losing no time, the
United States and Britain assigned specialist intelligence
teams to Pilsen, to take a look at Skoda's technical secrets
before the Red Army took over.[1] The project was kept under wraps, and no subsequent announcement of the mission was made at the time. The unexpected chance to look
backstage provided a one-time opportunity to probe how
far Skoda's eight-year technical cooperation with Germany's steel and arms giant Krupp had enriched the manufacturing processes of the Pilsen complex, which was ceded
to the Reich in 1938.

In view of Skoda's imminent absorption into the Soviet
arms industry, the intelligence information the two Allied
technical missions sought was vital. Skoda's steel-making,
gun-manufacturing, and gun-barrel-casting know-how was
legendary in its own right, as was its research and development operation. The U.S. and British intelligence teams
were also to look at Skoda's tank production, its gear-cutting shop, the foundry, rolling mill, and machine-tool

workshops.[2] Apart from Skoda's imminent potential for the Soviet armament industry, its impending emergence as Russia's partner in international heavy engineering projects was another reason for obvious U.S. and British interest. It should be borne in mind that Skoda's credits include participation in the building of the water turbine infrastructure of Niagara Falls, the Suez Canal, and scores of turnkey projects for Iran, China, and other countries.

The Allied intelligence teams were not aware of the topsecret SS research think tank operation that had been conducted under cover of Skoda's central research operations. The Soviets did have an inkling of the operation. But their undercover informants, who had established the penetration points, had failed to infiltrate the triple SS ring of military, industrial, and political counterintelligence staffs Himmler had assigned to Pilsen to protect the blueprints, the data, and the men who produced the research.

The Soviet informers were part of the technical intelligence organization Moscow had set up in 1944, to collect and analyze all technical information on captured German equipment. These expert teams accompanied the Red Army wherever it fought. Their staff work was so thorough that some teams assigned to captured factories already had complete lists of products they were interested in, even the names of key technical personnel. This information proved invaluable in the postwar dismantling operations. The bonanza of Skoda's pending acquisition was a much coveted plum for the Soviets, whose technicians had invariably accompanied their negotiating teams to Pilsen until 1941.

Despite Speer's all-out effort to keep Skoda in his bailiwick, Himmler succeeded in virtually turning it into an SS operation, with Kammler as one of his main go-betweens. To preempt major interservice rivalry, Voss, as its president, maintained a diplomatic lip service to Himmler. In a progress report in July 1942, when Skoda had completed development of a new, very accurate bomb, Voss sent his report to Himmler before putting it through respected channels. Field Marshal Erich Milch, then in charge of all aircraft production, should have been the first to get the report. Conscious of the in-fighting that was going on all around him at every twist and turn, Voss added a rider to the letter requesting Himmler's "permission" to pass on the report to Milch.

Later, in a letter marked TOP SECRET (March 30, 1942) Voss thanked Himmler for his initiative in obtaining Hitler's authority to channel all new weapons development, research, and production for the Waffen SS to Skoda. He added that he was striving to fulfill "all wishes," especially the wishes of the Waffen SS, "in every respect." Himmler was so pleased with the "smooth cooperation between Skoda and the Waffen SS" that, in a letter on May 8, 1942, he informed Voss that he was setting up a special Waffen SS liaison staff at Skoda's main office in Prague and that he was putting Voss in charge.

The new direct link to the "Reichsführer SS" at the führer headquarters was immediately underscored by the appearance of a brand-new letterhead reading, "Waffen SS Liaison Staff to the Skoda and Brünn Weapons Manufacturers at the General Management Offices of Skoda, in Prague." To conform with the fact that the link to the Waffen SS was now official, Voss signed all his letters as *Standartenführer SS* ("Colonel SS") from then on.

By the time the U.S. intelligence team was able to begin work at Skoda, the foretaste of the Cold War and the impending ringing down of the Iron Curtain had become more than evident. In Berlin, the Russians were making excuse after excuse for refusing access to the designated U.S. military detachment team to the American sector of the quadripartite city and kept the detachment out for almost two months. The changing political climate had completely permeated the atmosphere at Pilsen, seriously frustrating the work of the Allied missions. They had, as it turned out, been overly naive in their assumption that the wartime cooperation and support both countries had extended to the exiled Czechoslovak government and their liaison staffs on both sides of the Atlantic would be matched by a semblance of reciprocity now that their common enemy had been smashed.

The atmosphere at Pilsen not only reflected the spirit of the Czech-Soviet alliance of 1943/1944, which robustly put the country into the Soviet orbit long before the war was won, but fully bore out an American OSS intelligence analysis circulating at SHAEF and in emígré Czech government circles in London in January 1945. According to the analysis, the OSS had found "almost unanimous agreement among emígré Czechoslovak circles (in the United States) on the necessity and desirability of cooperation with the U.S.S.R." It went on to say that Czech Communist circles and left-wing Social Democrats were "willing and anxious to see Czechoslovakia more or less completely integrated with and dependent on Soviet policy." Ironically, the OSS analysis, showing the hand of the KGB, its wartime partner, summed up with the categoric conclusion that Czech "emígrés are convinced that the U.S.S.R will not impose either the economic nor political methods of Russian Communism on Czechoslovakia."[3]

Under the changed political climate, the Allied missions found themselves at the receiving end of humiliating stonewalling and general noncooperation at Skoda. Because of the nonavailability of relevant American documents, there is no record of the U.S. team's reaction to the runaround, nor its report to Washington. Two British intelligence reports, prepared for the Combined Intelligence Objective Committee, more than speak for themselves.

The reports, made available to the author by the Imperial War Museum Archives in London, leave no doubt that the obstructionist treatment meted out to the British missions had the sole purpose of preventing Skoda-Krupp military technology from falling into U.S. or British hands before all available data at the plant could be handed over to the Red Army. Present at Pilsen at the handing over of the Skoda Works to the Red Army on May 12, Lieutenant Colonel James Brierley, Chief of the first British intelligence mission to the Skoda Works, reported:

> Officials of the Skoda Works claimed that buildings which housed their drawings had been completely demolished together with their contents and therefore they could produce no drawings of their development projects. . . . Conversation with one of their lesser employees indicated that the firm had made microfilms of all their drawings, both standard and development items and these files had been stored in a safe place outside Pilsen.

The Skoda managers claimed that they had no knowledge whatever of microfilms and refused to discuss the topic any further. Britain's attempt to get an insight into Skoda's wartime gun, tank, and steel production had remained abortive. Subsequent high-level requests to Prague for the release of copies of the microfilms remained unanswered. The late-in-the-day request for this information underscores the fact that Britain had been unable to infiltrate the German-run plant in the face of the highly efficient SS counterintelligence screen in operation there. In an indirect reference to the SS counterintelligence operation, Brierley's report noted that it was his understanding that the SS screen was so effective that all sensitive test data or assembly of secret equipment was exclusively handled by SS technicians, or sent to Germany, to prevent sabotage and leakage.

The second British mission spent four days in Pilsen during September from the 22 to 25, and received the same runaround. Its civilian head, H.G. Barber, reported:

> In meeting with the General Manager of Skoda, its English speaking Commercial Manager and two Czech military officers employed to conduct visitors around the works, we were only met with excuses of why technical information on Skoda's wartime operations was not available. Extensive bomb damage was the usual excuse.[4]

The Czech Skoda managers fully succeeded in protecting their bailiwick. They guarded it as fiercely as a romantic hero guards his mistress. Brierly's final report bore this out.[5] His specific request for information on machine tools for gun rifling, on methods of casting steel for gun barrels, on the sophisticated optical measuring instruments Skoda used in its research department were simply not fulfilled. The Skoda staff invariably claimed that "all equipment and records" had been destroyed and burnt in recent air raids. Information was also withheld on experimental development work on small caliber missiles produced elsewhere. The U.S. teams was understood to have secured two of these missiles and data.

Undaunted, Brierly still hoped that his recommendation for the "dispatch of further investigators to Skoda, the attachment of a U.S. ordnance expert to the next British mission," and his suggestion that "Skoda should be instructed to prepare" organization charts of its weapons development department, might have some chance of bearing fruit. It was a further example of the type of political naiveté prominently found in the West at war's end, to the delight of the corner-cutting, go-getter Soviets.

Capping the runaround dealt the British intelligence teams combing through the spinoffs of German technology was the crudely stage-managed sudden "unavailability" of transportation to a number of listed Skoda subsidiaries, the inspection of which was requested by the second British intelligence mission in September. By that time all the Skoda subsidiaries were in Soviet hands, and fully operational. They included an undamaged underground gun factory, several plants producing machine tools, Diesel engines, electrical equipment, industrial plants, motor car production as well as shipyards on the Danube.

Under its new management, Skoda had already begun to build submarine propellers for the Red Navy and had started work on hydrofoils. A prototype, an eighty-four-foot craft propelled by two 2,500-horsepower engines, was being built by captured German naval architects, according to a former Skoda engineer who had succeeded in fleeing to the United States.

Between the first and second British intelligence missions to Pilsen, the shift of emphasis in East-West relations had visibly changed. Preoccupation with Communism had become a full-time task by September. Communists on whom both the United States and Britain had relied during the war had suddenly become openly hostile. The parting of the ways was just around the corner.

U.S. intelligence officers, returning to Europe from brief Washington attachments, had begun to alert their teams that the "next target" would be the Russians. Relations between Western and Soviet military personnel in the principal political, military, and occupation centers of Europe had also cooled.[6] By then, Continental nationals who had served the Allies during the war had also become aware that the undercover work they had put in did not, as they had taken for granted, guarantee automatic residence in the United States or Britain. Many thereafter opted to play safe, and openly collaborate with the Soviets, if it suited them.

Aware of the problem, U.S. and British intelligence officers were specifically instructed not to make any promises. They were directed not to recruit agents without carefully considering how to break off relations when an agent's usefulness ended. From then on, Czech refugees to the West were carefully screened before being granted asylum.

EIGHT

FAILED MISSION

> He who is bold enough to forge the
> brilliant red-gold treasure at the bot-
> tom of the Rhine into a ring, will
> have unlimited power over the Uni-
> verse.
>
> RICHARD WAGNER, *Das Rheingold*

THE COMBAT-WORN, dual-purpose, antiaircraft guns that for years had protectively ringed the giant Skoda Armament Works in the western outskirts of Pilsen had been unmanned for four days, since the city and plant had fallen to the U.S. Third Army on May 6. The skyward-pointing, sleek flak barrels, suggesting the raised arms of surrendering troops, seemed eerily in tune with the facts of defeat.

On that May 10, two days after the German surrender, the streets of Pilsen and the roads that radiated to Nuremberg in the west and Prague in the east were jam-packed with civilian and army convoys. Amid the heavy traffic, an unostentatious car wound its way through the potholed streets toward the bomb-scarred Skoda Works. The driver of the car was Dr. Wilhelm Voss, former president of Skoda. He was on a dangerous mission. The memory of his self-imposed mission remained clearly etched in his mind in 1949, when in several extended note-taking sessions with me, he recalled the chain of events that led to the loss to the Soviets of a truckload of high technology and vital-to-the-West research secrets.

"I had hoped that I would be able to convince the American officers in charge of the plant, pending its handing over to the Red Army, that a saving of whatever could be saved of the very advanced research data and blueprints was a matter of prime importance to American national defense. Once the material had fallen into Soviet hands, all this technology would obviously become a threat to Western security."

Voss went on to explain that his several official missions for Skoda to Moscow during the war—before the German invasion of Russia in 1941 had broken off relations—had given him an insight into the Soviet's unquenchable thirst for modernizing their military machine. It was a fair guess that the Soviets has a good idea of the booty they could expect on taking over Skoda.

As he appproached the Skoda complex, on May 10, 1945, Voss hoped that some members of the SS research operation he and Kammler had set up would still be around. The Third Reich had officially ended May 7. The unconditional surrender was signed by the defeated generals (instead of politicians, as the Versailles Treaty was) on May 8 and 9. Though the provisional post-Hitler government of Grand Admiral Karl Doenitz was officially still in office, it was impotent. The victors "did not deign to notice it," Speer, a member of that Cabinet, wrote later. To the world, U.S. President Harry Truman's declaration of May 8 as Victory Day in Europe (VE Day) was a reminder that the war was not yet over in the Pacific.

In undertaking the high-risk mission to Pilsen, Voss was fully aware that his former position at Skoda and as head of the Central Armaments division of the Reich Armaments and War Production Ministry under Speer, made him an automatic arrestee both in the Western and Eastern zones of Germany and in Czechoslovakia as well. Technically his word ceased to be law at Skoda[1] on January 27, 1945, when Goering, his superior as national war economy coordinator, summarily dismissed him for refusing to accept two nominees as plenipotentiaries on the Skoda Board. Voss had also been barred from the Skoda site, but he hoped that his excellent past relations with his former Czech codirectors and staff would at least help him obtain permission to enter the plant and open the way for an unobtrusive talk with the American officers now in control.

In his mind's eye, as he drove past the rotten row of flak guns, Voss recalled the mile-long row of solid bronze lamp posts lining Berlin's resplendent *Ost-West Achse* ("East-West Axis") Boulevard. He used to pass them on his way to his office at the Speer ministry on Pariser Platz, overlooking the Brandenburg Gate. He wondered if he would ever see them again, he said as he reminisced in 1949.[2]

The end of the Third Reich did not give him an "open sesame" to the Skoda Works, which, at best, would only remain in American hands for a few days. Since the bloody and brutal uprising of the Czech partisans in Prague on May 5 and with the fall of the Czech capital anticipated at any time, Voss expected the Red Army to reach Pilsen before long.

For weeks, he said, he had been monitoring foreign news bulletins, to pick the right time for his mission. The news flash on May 6, that Pilsen and Skoda had been captured by the Americans, had decided him. As soon as he could, he was underway to Pilsen from Votice, south of Prague, where he and his family had been occupying a hunting lodge on a Skoda estate, once the home of the manager of the brewery on the property.

Voss was hopeful, he said, that Kammler would have the same idea and was either headed for Pilsen or perhaps was already there to exploit the short breathing space available

BLUNDER!

before the Red Army took over. There was no way he could get in touch with Kammler. Through Wehrmacht contacts, he had learned that Kammler had transferred a group of the Peenemunde scientists to Bavaria shortly before the Americans took Nordhausen in April. He was also aware that the United States was in the process of evacuating a number of rockets and jet engines from the site before the plant and the provinces of Saxony and Thuringia were due to be handed over to the Soviets.

Voss explained that, not until news came of the unexpected U.S. military presence in Czechoslovakia, did it occur to him that there still might be an opportunity to save the research secrets along the lines the Americans followed at Nordhausen. As he approached the Skoda gates and the high-rise chimneys behind them, Voss felt suddenly full of fear. Vivid impressions and reflections still lingered in his memory four years later, as shown by the extensive notes the author was able to take at the time.

To a man who until recently was chief executive of Skoda, the thought of possibly having to ask for permission to enter the plant was humiliating. He recounted: "I had no idea what sort of reception would be in store for me. The Czech management and staff no longer had any loyalty to Germany, and I myself had no personal authority."

Despite his directorship of a number of enterprises in Czechoslovakia, Austria, and Italy, Voss had always regarded himself "first and foremost a Skoda man," he later told American interrogation officers at Nuremberg.[3] During our meetings in 1949, Voss recalled how his nervousness reached a peak when he drew up in front of the Skoda gates. There were some U.S. and German Army trucks around. Luckily the gate guard recognized Voss immediately. Ignoring a GI on duty alongside him, he signaled Voss to drive through, but Voss saw him pick up a telephone. Within minutes a young Czech appeared and escorted Voss to the wing where the executive offices were located.

Obviously Voss did not expect the type of reception he normally rated in the old days. Then he had had personal assistants and secretaries. The Section Chiefs "Referente" from the commercial and military side of the operation, reporting on the status of work in the gun and gear-cutting shops, the foundry, and the research division whose funding was channeled through him. Then came the accountants.

Throughout this visit, Voss was escorted. On his way to the office building, he had quite a shock. He had not realized how badly Skoda had been damaged, most of it during two massive raids on April 17 and 25. En route Voss spotted some Americans. He was anxious to make contact. His English was fluent, but he had no chance to talk to them then. Yet his hopes rose that he would soon get a chance to persuade them to take charge of the Kammler Group documents, as soon as he had pinpointed their whereabouts.

During his subsequent chat with the Czech managers, the difficulties confronting him on his self-imposed mission first dawned on him. The Czech management was firmly loyal to the future Czech government. To make things worse, the veteran Czech managers and engineers with whom he had run Skoda over the years were no longer around. Voss was glad to learn that, because of their decades-long loyalty to the Reich and their predictable fate should they fall into Russian hands, Hitler had provided them with last-minute facilities to cross into the American zone of Germany to surrender to the U.S. Army. Many had close links to the United States.

Voss suddenly realized that he had no hope of making headway with the Americans at the plant unless he knew exactly where the research documents were located. There was only a million-to-one chance that he might come across

[83]

someone in the know, someone he could trust. On his way out of the office wing, Voss was hailed by one of the designers who had worked in the Kammler Group and later had a chance for a private chat with the man.

Voss learned that his contact and two undercover members of the SS counterintelligence group who had maintained their cover had the same idea and had already formulated plans to get the research material into the U.S. zone of Germany. A selection of the most important documents and data had already been crated and loaded into a truck. The truck was parked close to the administration building. Its papers described the cargo as "Personnel and Payroll Records."

Voss also heard that some of the ordnance development blueprints had been microfilmed some time before the collapse was imminent, and the films had been evacuated by the Czech management. So far their exact location was not known to his informant. His contact and his two helpers had already made an attempt to get the truck out of the plant, but called it off when they found it could not be managed at the time.

Voss then decided to take the bull by its horns. It was high time to see the American officer in charge.[4] Now that Voss knew the location of the research material he felt he had a stronger hand. The officer listened to Voss, then flatly turned thumbs down on the whole project. His instructions were to hand over everything to the Red Army, and he meant *everything.* This was their designated zone. Everything at Skoda was to be kept for them, and it was his job to see that this was done.

Voss explained carefully who he was, why he had risked his life to come to Pilsen. He told the officer that before the war he had maintained very close contacts with the U.S. and British armament industries, and it was in the *urgent interest* of the United States that the key research documents should be prevented from falling into Soviet hands.

Disregarding the cold-shouldering, Voss persisted, pointing out that the American officer need not have any qualms over helping to save the material, as an American ordnance team was in the process at Nordhausen of preparing captured missiles and aeroengines for shipment to the United States. Such an obviously major operation could not be mounted without Washington's authority, and Washington would obviously also approve his actions, if they were aware what it was all about.

Voss, a veteran of the arms trade and Army red tape, was on the right track. He could not have been aware of the U.S. Joint Chiefs of Staff Directive 1064 of April 24, 1945. It, in fact, directed American military personnel to "preserve from destruction and take under your control all records, plans, notes, documents, scientific information and data, belonging to German organizations engaged in military research."

The American officer was adamant. He was not prepared to break regulations. He had nothing to do with intelligence. Besides, an American ordnance team had already inspected the plant earlier that week and had taken two rocket missiles they had found on the proving grounds. Obviously they had picked up "all they needed," the officer told Voss.

Voss tried once more. He told the officer that the crated documents represented vital-to-the-Western-military-research material developed by a top group of scientists and designers. They should be rushed across the border to the U.S. zone of Germany and handed to the nearest U.S. Army headquarters before the plant was handed over to the Russians, who were nowhere near at the time. Voss urged the officer not to regard the material as part of the Skoda inventory the U.S. holding group was to hand over to the Red Army.

The officer remained unimpressed and immovable. He did not "want to know anything" about an undercover SS research operation at Skoda. It wasn't his job to worry about it. The war was over. He and his men hoped to be on their way home soon and were not going to waste any time checking through or moving "any damn crates."

Voss got nowhere. He was still fuming with indignation over the impasse when he recalled the Pilsen events to me, some four years later. "It was criminal stupidity. The officer was very much aware that it was an intelligence matter and that he was under orders to alert the nearest intelligence HQ to seek instructions. His refusal even to hear me out came as a terrible shock. I had assumed that an American officer would show more common sense than a Wehrmacht officer would have under similar circumstances. But, remember, to him I was just a German, we had just lost the war, he did not have to listen to me, or take me by my word."

Voss spent the night at the plant and witnessed the handover to the Red Army two days later, on May 12. That morning he spotted a British Army staff car, which had just arrived with a group of officers. He was told that it was a British military mission assigned to inspect the workshop and the plant. Voss realized that there would be no chance to make contact. Just then, as part of the handover, the Skoda motor pool and a number of German Army trucks were being split into several groups. Suddenly Voss spotted his contact, who with his two companions was sauntering toward the truck with the crated research documents. Looking very casual, they boarded the truck and began to roll toward the U.S. Army motor pool, which was not involved in the handing-over operation. An alert GI spotted the ploy and waved them back.

An equally alert Red Army transport officer was quick on the uptake. He signaled the truck to pull up, and ordered its three occupants to step down. The truck was unloaded. One of the crates was pried open. Seconds later, the three men who almost saved the research documents for the West were marched away under the point of a Russian machine pistol.

Voss recalled that it was at this point he realized just how miserably his mission had failed. The golden nest egg he had tried to save would now be on its way into the maws of the technology-hungry Soviet war machine. "It was the most negative mission of my life," Voss recalled in 1949.

Having witnessed the handover of the Skoda Works to the Red Army and the irretrievable loss of the SS research secrets he had come to prevent from ending up in Soviet hands, Voss decided that it was high time to end his abortive self-imposed mission, and to head for home. Suddenly, he recalled later, he spotted several Czech members of the Kammler Group in the proceess of boarding a string of staff cars lined up near the administration building. He knew them all, yet none of the group made any sign of recognition.

Probably they represented the vanguard of the bulk of the Kammler team, which had opted to remain in the Soviet sphere of influence. They would either take up residence in Czechoslovakia or move to the Soviet Union, to resume research under the optimum working and financial conditions they had been offered within the Soviet armament industry which was far from exhausted at that juncture.

In fact the exodus of the Kammler experts from Pilsen represented only the tip of the iceberg of the eastward drain of the cream of Third Reich scientific manpower that Moscow culled from the Soviet zones of Germany and Austria. These were part of the team that had made such an astounding record for the Third Reich before, during, and in the later stages of the war. The Peenemunde group of rocket makers around Dr. Wernher von Braun, who laid the groundwork for the U.S. moon landing program, represented only a fraction of the Reich's technical know-how.

As the staff cars pulled out from the Skoda grounds, the German general who had handled the German end of the handover told Voss he had just received a report that Kammler had committed suicide by taking cyanide on May 9, in a "forest between Pilsen and Prague." There was no way Voss could check the report and whether it had come from an eyewitness. Nor was Voss ever able to find out whether General Kammler had managed to slip into the plant before it was captured by the U.S. Army on May 6.

The flood of questions remained unanswered. And there was no time to ponder. Voss realized that the longer he stayed, the greater the danger of being picked up by the Russians, if they found out who he was. It was a miracle no one had already denounced him.

As he headed for his car, a Czech Skoda employee he vaguely knew came up to him and asked if he might have a lift to Prague, aware that Voss had to go past Prague on his way home, all other roads being hopelessly jammed. Voss readily agreed. In case of roadblocks a Czech passenger would be just as well. On reaching Prague, his passenger asked to be taken to the sprawling Skoda main office in Jungmann Strasse, in the heart of Prague. The building came through the war with little damage.

The city, however, still showed every sign of the siege. Red Army tanks were everywhere, sprawling across city squares and guarding their bridges across the Moldau River. Anti-German graffiti were ubiquitous. At their destination Voss pulled up, then got out of the car to stretch his legs before driving on. He did not intend to enter the building.

Suddenly two plainclothesmen came out of the office block. "Dr. Voss?" one asked. Voss nodded. He was asked to follow and was shown to an inside office. Then a senior Czech officer entered. He told Voss he would be detained to probe his wartime record and whether he had participated in any activity that would make him liable for trial under Czech laws. Voss nodded in acknowledgment, resigned to his fate. He rightly guessed he would be taken to a prison rather than an internment camp. He asked at once if he could telephone his wife. The officer shook his head in silence. Then he spoke hesitantly. "I'm sorry. I have some very sad news for you. We did not want to phone you when we heard you were at Pilsen. An armed group of bandits on an anti-German rampage in Votice has swooped down on your home and caused great damage."

He hesitated again, unable to look Voss in the face. Then he added slowly, "It seems there were no survivors."

If at any time in his life Voss was near suicide, it was that minute, he recalled in 1949.

VARIATIONS ON A THEME

This time it vanished quite slowly beginning with the end of the tail and ending with a grin, which remained some time after the rest of it had gone.

LEWIS CARROLL, *Alice in Wonderland*

ON MAY 9, 1945, a Wednesday, all hostilities had officially ceased in the European Theater of Operations. The surrender of all German forces everywhere went into effect at 0001 hours. In Prague, Czech patriots used the last few hours before the expected arrival from Dresden of the Red Army's first Ukrainian Front to vent their pent-up venom against anything German.

The piecemeal negotiations for the German capitulation were in their tenth day. They had opened in Italy on April 29, the day before Hitler's suicide. They followed negotiations with the Allies by Waffen SS General Karl Wolff. Fighting in Italy had come to an end on May 2, the day Berlin surrendered to the Red Army.

In northern Germany, the government of Hitler-appointed successor Grand Admiral Karl Doenitz had much facilitated winding up the surrender. It provided a supreme commander to whom the Wehrmacht could transfer the personal oath of allegiance it had once given to Hitler and a head of state with whom the Allies could negotiate. The signatories acted under the authority of Doenitz.

In Prague, it had been open season on Germans since May 5, the day partisans of the 30,000-man home army rose to end the last vestiges of the German occupation. Prague City Hall, seat of the Nazi administration, was blown up by partisan tanks early that week. Meanwhile Field Marshal Ferdinand Schoerner's Panzer Army and its three tough SS divisions showed no sign of giving way and continued to pin down the Red Army some seventy kilometers east of Prague.

At that time, by quirk of circumstances, Schoerner was Commander in Chief of the German Army, a historic fact generally unchronicled in postwar histories. His appointment arose under Hitler's political testament of April 29, one day before his suicide. Until that day, Hitler himself held the command, which he had assumed in December 1941, after he dismissed Field Marshal Walther von Brauchitsch. In his will, Hitler also named Schoerner as a member of the Reich Cabinet his successor, Grand Admiral Karl Doenitz, was to form. Schoerner was one of three persons designated to receive copies of Hitler's political testament, which was sent to him into the field through a liaison officer.

Because of the uprising of the Czech partisans in Prague and the greater part of Bohemia and Moravia, Schoerner's Army Group Center delayed compliance with the capitulation deadline set for 0.00 hours on May 9. Communications to units had broken down. The partisans had been embittered that their radio appeal to the West, begging for relief against Schoerner's SS troops, had been ignored—as they rightly suspected, on political grounds.

In Prague, marauding partisans and armed bandits had been on a bloody rampage, wrecking German property and routing out Schoerner's SS troops and the anti-Soviet Vlasov troops. The partisans daubed swastikas on the backs of collaborators. Many were grotesquely tortured before being put to death. Eyewitnesses reported that soon lamp posts were festooned with the mutilated bodies of collaborators, their abdomens bayoneted and slashed upwards to their full lengths.

On May 9, some hours after the surrender had been in effect, an armed Russian patrol passing a bombed-out building spotted a solid iron door barring the entrance to a cellar and decided to investigate. A burst of bullets, drumming against the shell-pocked door, almost lifted it from its hinges. A further fusillade of fire finished off the crippled door. The cellar indeed turned out to be a German hideout, packed with some twenty to twenty-five SS troops. They came out fighting. There was an SS general among them. Firing his machine pistol, he emerged laughing, reports circulating after the war claimed. Suddenly a volley of bullets rang out from behind the general. The shots came from the machine pistol of an officer just a few paces behind him. The salvo hit the nape of the general's head, pulping it into a bloody mess. The officer who had aimed the shots himself succumbed at once to a hail of partisan fire.

A wounded SS survivor gave the general's name as Hans Kammler. The officer who fired the shots that killed the general was stated to be his adjutant, reportedly *SS Obersturmbannführer* Starck. This highly colored, dramatic account of Kammler's death at the hand of his adjutant in the heart of Prague, the day before the Czech capital was taken by the Red Army, appears to have received ready acceptance when it was relayed to London during Dornberger's interrogation.

There is only one basic fact wrong with the report. It happens to be one of *four* versions that have come to light since Kammler dropped out of sight in Munich on April

17, 1945. Three of the four reports, to be analyzed in depth later, alleged that Kammler's death had occured in Czechoslovakia, and uniformly put the date of death as May 9, the coincident official end of the Third Reich. But the fourth version, claiming just as much authenticity, suggests that Kammler had died in April, in Austria, thus pre-dating his death before that of his leader, whose suicide on April 30 was not announced until May 1.

Intriguingly, the locale of the fourth version is given as Ebensee, near Gmunden, Salzkammergut in upper Austria. Two years previously Kammler had tunneled an underground bombproof aircraft and missile factory site there, into the chalk caves of the Hochkogl and Erlakogel mountain range overlooking Traunsee Lake. It was to serve as a second alternate evacuation site for the Peenemunde rocket group, should Nordhausen be overrun before it could be made operational.

The SS construction office (C Division), which Kammler headed, maintained a regional office at Ebensee, run by a deputy until the last day of the war, official documents show.

The existence of four conflicting versions of Kammler's death stepped up the mystery of what really happened to the man only recently regarded the "most important man in Germany outside the Cabinet" and only twice removed from Hitler. (As of 1944, when Himmler's deputy, SS General Karl Wolff, assumed the command of all SS and police troops in Italy, only SS General Oswald Pohl stood between Kammler and Himmler.) The first version—death by cyanide at his own hand—came to my attention during a series of exclusive background interviews I had with Voss in Frankfurt and Bavaria in 1949. The interview was conducted in the process of researching a syndicated news feature on the wartime role of Skoda as an arms maker for the Reich.

I had first heard of Kammler in a marginal reference, while covering the war crimes trials of several leading German armament industry executives in Nuremberg, some of whom, including some Skoda board members, were later convicted.

Details of the SS think tank operation were spelled out to me by Voss in in-depth background briefings in Frankfurt and at his home at Rottach-am-Tegernsee, near Munich, early in 1949. He also summarized the highlights in writing. But on March 30, 1949 Voss wrote requesting that the "hot matter" (*die heisse Angelengenheit*) we had discussed was not for publication.

Voss stated that he had given the full story of the secrets leakage at Pilsen and Kammler's disappearance to U.S. intelligence in West Germany but was told at highest level to keep the matter under wraps, along with the briefings he then gave U.S. intelligence of the areas covered by the SS research in Pilsen. This clampdown meant that the author could not make use of the story at the time.

Voss said that he had first heard Kammler's suicide story on May 12, 1945, while at Pilsen, and that the date of the suicide was put as May 9. The gist of the story as related to him then pinpointed the suicide in a forest between Prague and Pilsen, which are about fifty kilometers apart. Kammler had been accompanied by some SS troops. A short drive from Pilsen, Kammler halted the car and walked into a copse. When his absence appeared overlong, his adjutant attempted to trace his whereabouts. After a while he had found Kammler's body. Between his teeth Kammler had a crushed cyanide capsule. He was buried on the spot. A member of the group then made contact with a Skoda employee.

This version later came up during the 1958 trial of a group

of officers and noncommissioned officers accused of carrying out Kammler's alleged order for the decimating of mostly Russian and Polish workers attached to Kammler's rocket group during the retreat of the V-1 operation from Holland in 1945. Trial records, made available to the author by the German authorities, show that three mass executions had taken place involving the death of 129 men, 77 women, and 2 children.[1]

The determination of the date of Kammler's death then became relevant. An eyewitness was called who claimed to have buried Kammler's body in a "makeshift grave" after finding traces of "broken glass" between his lips. The witness, whose name is blocked out in the court records but is known to the author from other sources, held the rank of *SS Untersturmbannführer* ("lieutenant") in 1945. During the trial, he told the court he had served as "Kammler's adjutant from Christmas 1944 to the day he died" between Pilsen and Prague. Neither name nor rank of the witness tally with that of *SS Obersturmbannführer* ("Lieutenant Colonel") Starck, identified as Kammler's adjutant by his former associates, V-2 developers General Walter Dornberger and Wernher von Braun.

My notes, taken during my talk with Voss in 1949, do *not* indicate that I had attached any great significance to the Kammler suicide story. It could not be known that it would be a forerunner to *three* further contradictory versions of his death. The notes show that Voss was not at all convinced of the authenticity of the story, the sole version of Kammler's purported death, at the time. He was very skeptical. He said he felt it was hard to believe that a man of Kammler's caliber, a brilliant executive in his early forties, and at the peak of his career, would accept defeat that easily. Anyone who had the know-how to design and build an underground aircraft factory and handle the type of major civil-engineering jobs Kammler handled would have been welcomed with open arms by an underdeveloped country. His political past would be of no consequence.

Voss's legal advisers, who looked after his interest while he was a witness at Nuremberg, later told the author they tended to share Voss's view. So did a prominent German jurist, who had familiarized himself with Kammler's career during the 1958 war-crimes trial of members of his former staff. He had expressed his skepticism at the time of the trial and confirmed his view in a recent talk with the author. The jurist feels that Kammler's qualifications would have landed him a top job in a dozen countries, "regardless of whether he carried secret research material in his knapsack," and there is every chance he did survive.

Kammler's purported death at the hands of a *coup de grace* administered by his adjutant in Prague is version two in the series of four stories of his death. Version three surfaced recently, in the course of correspondence and interviews with two of Kammler's wartime staff. The contact arose as a result of an advertisement the author had placed in the Waffen SS periodical *Der Freiwillinge* ("The Volunteer"), circulating among former members of the Waffen SS and other branches of the SS in Germany and abroad.[2] The advertisement brought considerable response: It read:

AUTHOR SEEKS INFORMATION
on the movements/death in April/May 1945 on V-weapons General-Plenipotentiary, Waffen-SS General Dr. Ing. Hans Kammler.

This version also places Kammler in Prague in early May, but the story differs in every respect from the *coup de grace* version of death at the hands of his adjutant. The vivid story, based on the recollections of two members of the Prague regional office of the Buildings and Works Division of the

SS Economic Main Office in Berlin, is relevant to the Kammler mystery.[3] In the words of one, a highly qualified civil engineer:

> Kammler arrived in Prague early May. We did not expect him. He gave no advance notice of his arrival. Nobody knew why he had come to Prague, when the Red Army was closing in.
>
> But we had the impression that he was on his way somewhere. He showed no interest in the Bureau, nor did he make use of the suite of offices at his disposal. By that time, most of the Czech population had turned against us. Even before the uprising, German women and collaborators were being brutalized, hanged on lamp posts or trees, or doused in petrol and set on fire as human torches.
>
> When news got around that the Czech appeal to the West would not be acted upon, the coming uprising was already in the air. Most of the German community still in Prague began to panic. Anyone who had access to liquor hit the bottle. Kammler remained calm, ignored the orgies and the defeatist *Heute Rot, Morgen Tot* (Red today, dead tomorrow) atmosphere. He even took time to educate his temporary *Offizierschbursche* (orderly) on how to stack his always highly polished high boots to stand upright. The man pleaded that it could not be done without *Stiefelspanner* (boot trees) and that *Herr General* had not brought any. Kammler smilingly set to and demonstrated how it could be done by turning the boots sideways, then propping them up against the wall.

The second Kammler aide took up the story from here:

> At dawn, on the 5th May, just as the Czech uprising was about to get going, Kammler paraded all available

[97]

fit German males. We were all issued small arms. Kammler said he had been tipped that a nearby Home Army arms cache was lightly guarded and that we were to try to blow it up. Leading the way with his informant, Kammler found the cache. The guard was killed, we blew up the arms and ammunition we found and retreated.

For the next three days, until the 8th, the general, myself and four others managed to hide out in the outskirts. Finally we managed to slip out of Prague. On the night of the 8th, having picked up a truck, we headed west. Kammler decided that we should try to spend the night at the SS Barracks at Ruzyn, a Prague suburb. But when we entered the barracks, we saw it was full of SS Vlasov troops.[4] True enough, they had fought well with the Waffen SS, but you know how it is when you don't like the look of someone. We just did not like the look of this lot. With the *Ivan* just around the corner, there was the risk the Vlasov lot might turn us in—especially the general—by way of reinsurance. An eleventh-hour repentant would stand a better chance than a Russian in SS uniform, especially if he has bagged a full Waffen SS general. So we left the Ruzyn Barracks and headed toward Eger (Cheb) on the German border, so as to give us a chance to slip across the border into the U.S. zone. The Red Army already held most of Czechoslovakia, and the war was over. Then near Karlsbad (Karlovy Vary), we ran across some Americans. We just managed to avoid them and slipped into the woods. It was out of the combat zone, there was no sign of the Red Army, so we bivouacked.

The next morning the general asked us to gather around him. It was to be a farewell speech. We stood to rigid attention as he told us that as the objectives the Führer had set could not be fulfilled he was relieving us of all duties and that we were free to go home.

Kammler then walked into the woods. Shortly after, we
heard a single shot. We chased after him, but it was too
late. He had shot himself with his service pistol. We
quickly buried him on the spot.

To round off the story, he was asked if he could recall
exactly how Kammler had died. Did he shoot himself in
the mouth, temple, or heart? Was he found lying on his
back, on his side when the source and his companions found
him shortly after hearing the shot? Was Kammler dead,
dying? If the latter, did anyone try to revive him?

Though endowed, as most Germans are, with almost total recall, the ex-Kammler aide, now in his late seventies,
was totally out of his depth and was unable to provide information. It was a strange gap in memory for veterans, especially as the information sought concerned the suicide
and burial of his commanding officer, by no means an event
one easily forgets.

Surprisingly, his memory was perfectly clear on other
matters, such as details of his group's escape from Prague,
capture by the U.S. Army, confinement at a U.S. Army
prisoner-of-war camp at Regensburg (U.S. zone, Germany),
transfer to the French as a prisoner-of-war civil-engineering worker, a subsequent three-year stint in Bordeaux,
building houses, private swimming pools and roads. He
reached home on October 10, 1948. So much for version
three.

Version four in the death of Kammler series came to light
in the course of a search of the German Red Cross search
service master files in Munich and cross-checks with the
Austrian Red Cross in Vienna. The Kammler dossier opens
with a routine registration of his name as a missing person
last heard of at Ebensee, Steiermark (Styria), Austria, in April
1945. The registration was filed by a relative in 1945.

The card details Kammler's personal particulars, showing his place of birth as Stettin on August 26, 1901, his last rank (general—Waffen SS), his last address as of September 1, 1959 (an address in Berlin, close to his office), and his civilian profession (construction engineering executive). It even lists his academic grade as Dr. Ing, Doctor Engineer.

The second document amends the original category of listing from "missing" to "dead" and cites the source of the report as "unnamed comrades," site Austria, date April. The information is incorporated in a third document, referred to by the Red Cross as its "Master File on General Officers." This card lists Kammler's status as "dead, according to statements of comrades," and again gives the date of the report as April 1945, site as Austria.

None of the three Red Cross documents substantiates Kammler's death, nor pinpoints the exact date of death. There is no indication of a burial place. The Red Cross makes no bones about the fact that the documentation is totally inconclusive and has called the author's attention to the fact that the "the comrades" listed as the source of the original 1945 report from Ebensee "have never been identified."

The Red Cross Secretariat General in Munich has also volunteered the information that the standard reference book the organization uses to help determine the wartime fate of general officers of all arms of the service *"most conspicuously"* omits mention of General Kammler's name at all.[5] The comprehensive reference book,[6] published in 1953, eight years after the war, lists all general officers reported as missing, or their death on active service, in captivity, by suicide, or by execution on conviction by a German or a foreign court-martial. The German War Graves Commission and various Waffen SS records consulted by the author likewise do *not* list Kammler's fate at all.

Equally curious is the fact that neither the Austrian Red Cross, which by coincidence has on file some correspondence relating to the last days of Kammler's office at Ebensee before the collapse, nor the local and provincial Austrian administration offices, specifically asked by the Red Cross main office in Vienna to assist, could locate any evidence of Kammler's presence at Ebensee in April 1945.

It would seem that like H.G. Wells's immortal *Invisible Man*, Kammler too had the knack of dropping out of sight as easily as Kemp, who did it simply by slipping out of his clothes. An additional mystery was inadvertently provided by the source of some of the background information in this chapter, a former Kammler aide. After a long session in Hamburg early in 1983, as I accompanied him to his train, and we had already bid each other *"Wiedersehen,"* I used the opportunity to fire one more question at him. Admittedly it was a curved one. I spoke just as his train was about to pull out.

"Tell me, what if Kammler suddenly made an appearance, say if he had just stepped off this train, spotted you, and hailed you with a hearty *'Wie geht's'*, how would you react?"

Subconsciously, he hastily scanned the faces on the platform, obviously forgetting that Kammler would be in his eighties if alive. My visitor's reaction was very prompt. With a smile he said, "To tell you the truth, it would not surprise me *one bit.*"

UNFINISHED FINALE

For want of a nail, the shoe was lost
For want of a shoe, the horse was lost
And for want of a horse, the rider was
lost.

BENJAMIN FRANKLIN

Aттемpting To Trace Kammler's movements after April 17, 1945, the day he was last heard of in Munich, is like searching for a missing aircraft last seen plowing through a cloud bank almost four decades before. The existence of four totally different accounts of his purported fate adds to the mystery.

Analysis of the voluminous documentation that has accrued since I embarked on the first leg of the fascinating project in 1949 shows crude discrepancies, the inconsistencies of which grow with almost every addition to the mosaic of information that enters the picture. Basically three major facts stand out:

1. In almost four decades, official records show *no* positive confirmation of Kammler's death. No court of law, no media editor would accept the uncorroborated statement of "unknown comrades," still so referred to in official records as conclusive evidence of death—especially if the death was alleged to have taken place in the chaos of collapsing Germany.

2. The record shows no subsequent sworn corroborative

statement. Such a statement would automatically have been entered in the Red Cross and other dossiers on Kammler.

3. None of the persons reporting any of the four versions of the general's death had conformed with the prescribed duty of all servicemen to detach one-half of a dead comrade's identity disc and forward it, along with the dead man's soldier's paybook or officer's identity document, to the nearest unit, relevant records office, Red Cross, or holding power, if the surviving serviceman had become a prisoner of war, to help notification of next of kin. Germans are traditionally meticulous and, to say the least, most sentimental in such matters.

Despite the proliferation of unsubstantiated evidence that permeates all four versions of Kammler's death, the shell of the case contains sufficient facts to suggest a more than coincidental pattern of seemingly targeted and organized disinformation. This was possibly motivated to cloud over the circumstances of Kammler's movements after April 17, 1945, when he last made contact with his Berlin headquarters.

The readiness to accept one version or another of Kammler's suicide, however unsubstantiated, may well be the product of like-oriented Nazi minds. To them the very thought of an SS general leaving the battle alive after his leader had fallen indeed spelled lifelong infamy and shame, as Tacitus put it.

Even Speer, who had hated Kammler since he had replaced Speer in Hitler's favor, appears to fall in with this theory. In Speer's last book, published shortly before his death in London in 1981, he refers to the account of Kammler's death in Prague, alleging that he had been shot on his own orders by his adjutant.[1] "Perhaps, after all, he had acted in elitist SS loyalty," Speer wrote.

By all means, *chacun à son goût*, but even the most ardent worshipper of Teutonic creed could not possibly suggest that elitist SS loyalty can be successfully demonstrated three times, in three locations, and all on the same day.

In 1949, when the Kammler story first aroused my interest, only one version of his purported death had circulated. It was the account Voss had related. It alleged that Kammler had killed himself with cyanide somewhere along the road between Pilsen and Prague on May 9.

The second version, which Speer cites, had surfaced during the post-surrender interrogation of General Walter Dornberger, who along with the evacuated core of the Peenemunde rocket group, had surrendered to the U.S. Army on May 2. The report of Kammler's death was said to have reached Dornberger through private channels.

It should be noted that the report on Kammler's death was of great personal interest to Dornberger, who had had an intense dislike of Kammler ever since 1944.

In August 1945, Dornberger and von Braun were flown to London for a ten-day period, to advise British rocket experts on the modalities of assembling and firing the batch of V-2s Britain was allotted by the United States from the captured V-2s it had acquired at Nordhausen. But while von Braun was allowed to return to Germany and was soon off with 120 members of the Peenemunde team on a permanent assignment to the United States, Dornberger was retained in Britain as a prisoner of war for two years, for technical questioning.

The *coup de grace* version of Kammler's purported death had apparently been accepted in Britain and conveniently closed the book on Kammler at a critical time. This suited both Dornberger and Britain, where signs were already multiplying that the man who had directed the indiscriminate V-weapon terror campaign, killing or wounding some 46,000 British civilians between September 8, 1944 and

March 27, 1945, should, if apprehended, be tried for war crimes. Had Kammler been located and brought to trial the British public might well have clamored for a hanging verdict as it did during World War I, when emotions were excited with the cry of "Hang the Kaiser." But Kammler was conveniently nowhere to be found.

While undergoing interrogation at the London Cage, headed by the legendary Colonel Alexander Scotland, Dornberger let it be known that, should Britain have in mind trying him as a surrogate for Kammler, then all other engineers, scientists, and designers of weapons of war—including the atom bomb—should be in the dock with him.[2] The subsequent slotting of the Peenemunde group into the U.S. missile program underscored even more the vast legal complexity trying Kammler would have presented to the Allies. The logic of this argument, also aired elsewhere, obviously had made an impact as in due course Dornberger was released by Britain. He later joined Bell Aerospace in the United States and became its vice president and chief scientific consultant.

Meanwhile there are two puzzling footnotes to the Kammler story, compounding the mystery even further. The mystery is rooted in sharply contrasting marginal references to Kammler, said to have been made by Dornberger and von Braun while undergoing interrogation by U.S. intelligence after the war. Both are recalled in a book by their interrogating officer James McGovern, who subsequently headed the CIA station in Berlin.

According to McGovern, Dornberger had the impression in late March 1945, shortly before the Peenemunde group evacuated Nordhausen for Oberammergau, that Kammler's "mental condition had rapidly worsened" and his "traditional overconfidence had swung over into self-doubt and nervousness."

Dornberger also reported overhearing Kammler's instructions to his adjutant, also before the move to Bavaria, that "should things become hopeless" at any time *SS Obersturmbannführer* Starck should "put a salvo of bullets into Kammler's head, wasting no more time."[3]

Intriguingly, Dornberger's reported assessment of Kammler's mental health as of late March 1945 is in sharp contrast with von Braun's report of having overheard a private conversation between Kammler and Starck a fortnight later in Oberammergau. In the course of that, the general and his adjutant reportedly discussed the possibility of going underground before the U.S. Army arrived, by taking refuge at the nearby Benedictine Ettal Abbey and donning the habit of the religious order as a disguise.

Most markedly, Kammler's name was not featured at the Nuremberg war crimes trials, despite his active involvement in the indictable offense of participation in the employment of slave labor, for which Speer served twenty years, and the decimation of Russian and Polish workers carried out under his alleged orders in 1945. Kammler was not tried in absentia, as was Martin Bormann, whose whereabouts were just as shrouded in speculation.

In fact, only once did Kammler's name come up during the Nuremberg war crimes trials. The occasion arose during Speer's interrogation on details of the guided missile program. The interrogator who conducted the session was the chief U.S. prosecutor, Justice Robert C. Jackson, on June 21, 1946. Fielding responsibility in this area, Speer referred to a "certain SS General Kammler" as having had command. Neither Speer, nor Justice Jackson, nor other members of the quadripartite prosecution team deemed it necessary to pursue the questioning in an attempt to bring into focus Kammler's policy-making role in several key Nazi bailiwicks.[4]

On this note, the Nuremberg tribunal closed its book on

Kammler. They little guessed that the man who at war's end had operational command of all forerunners of the full range of Cruise, Pershing, and SS-20 series of missiles—which were to form the backbone of the NATO and Warsaw Pact armories in the eighties—would become a four-time mystery man, whose disappearance raised a flock of questions that are still not answered. The International Military Tribunal was directly responsible for elbowing General Kammler into the news-shadow area in which he had reposed for four decades.

Intriguingly, although to some accounts he purportedly died and had been buried four times in 1945, there are no tombstones to Kammler's memory, *leaving four empty graves for the general.*

The unsolved mystery prompts a fresh look at Kammler's disappearance. In his position he had an inside knowledge of the progress in German scientific efforts in the military field and details of the desperate race the Germans were engaged in for the secrets of the atom and other very sophisticated military research. He had at his fingertips all the clues to the knowledge intelligence series sought on the ruins of the Reich as it gradually opened up to them.

Kammler was indeed a coveted trophy.

During the final two years of the war he had been moving up the SS executive ladder with a speed seldom matched even in the rarefied world of big business. There was no doubt in the mind of Third Reich insiders that their assessment of Kammler as the "most important man in Germany outside the Cabinet" exactly fitted this incurably inquisitive and ambitious man.

In 1943, this former unobtrusive construction engineer suddenly stepped into the limelight. He was no longer a faceless crowd artist on the bizarre stage of the Third Reich. His star was in the ascendancy. Everyone began to pander to his unmatched track record of accomplishment. To Hitler, Kammler was one of the last few in his entourage he thought he could trust and whose *yes* was not that of a man who agrees, but *in pectore* disagrees, but a firm pledge to tackle an assignment which to others appeared impossible. As a rule, Kammler succeeded admirably.

Over the short span of years, Hitler, Himmler, and Goering repeatedly threw their command machinery into high gear to skyrocket Kammler to a series of newly created key posts that gave him centralized influence and made him privy to the Reich's most sensitive military technical secrets.

In January 1943, rounding off the multifaceted authority he already held in the SS empire two rungs below Himmler in the *Schutzstaffel* pecking order, Goering picked him for the vital task of putting as many aircraft and missile production centers underground as time permitted.

The next promotion came from Himmler six months later when Kammler was given operational charge (as Deputy to SS General Oswald Pohl) of the entire V-2 construction program. This appointment turned out to be a forerunner of the SS infiltration of the armament industry and Kammler's eventual emergence as supreme commander of all German secret weapons, including the trailblazing Messerschmitt ME-262 jet fighter and its tactical squadrons.

Kammler already held de facto command of the Reich's concentration camp and convict labor force, as well as a very senior voice in running the Gestapo.

Then, in one of the most subtle examples of targeted infiltration of Armament Minister Albert Speer's bailiwick, Himmler appointed Kammler as "Special SS Expediter for the Armament Industry." This foothold was soon pyramided into yet another key assignment—this time as deputy to Paul Pleiger, all powerful managing board chairman of the vast "Reich Hermann Goering Works" industrial complex, comprising the Skoda Works and its affiliated plants. This part of the assignment was much publicized.

The fact that Himmler assigned Kammler for the covert job of setting up a top-secret SS research think tank operation at Pilsen, strictly behind the backs of both Goering and Speer, *was kept under wraps.*

The Command Order of March 27, 1945, making Kammler Supreme Commander of the entire ME-262 production program, subordinating both Goering and Speer in this sector, was signed by Hitler in the dank, dark warren of his Command Bunker, fourteen meters below the Reich Chancellory, just five weeks before he finally threw in the towel and took his own life, on April 30.

ELEVEN

PHOENIX

After the deluge the Phoenix is born.
JEAN DE LA FONTAINE

WHILE THE INTERNATIONAL Military Tribunal firmly closed the book on Kammler, it far from closed the book on Voss. Though never indicted, he was considered a vital witness on the inner workings of the Krupp affiliate, Skoda. He little guessed that his inside knowledge, expertise, and standing in the international arms trade, unmarred by his association with the top echelon of the Third Reich, would before long catapult him into screaming headlines on both sides of the Atlantic, when he assumed a key role in the erupting volcano of the Middle East.

Voss was in a highly stressful state in mid-1946 over the unpredictability of his future. On the first of several hundred nights he served as an automatic arrestee in the bomb-scarred Nuremberg Palace of Justice prison. He tossed about sleepless in his bunk, nervous under the single naked overhead bulb that never went out. He had just been repatriated from Czechoslovakia, where he had been held for interrogation since the day he was detained in Prague on May 12, 1945.[1]

Other wings in the sprawling gray complex of the Palace of Justice held former associates Hermann Goering, Speer, Foreign Minister Joachim von Ribbentrop, Reich Protector of Bohemia and Moravia Constantin von Neurath, a frequent visitor to Skoda, and other top Third Reich leaders. They were undergoing the final stages of their trial as major war criminals before the International Military Tribunal, all awaiting a predicted possible death sentence on conviction.

Scores of others, whose names made less immediate news, were held in another cell block. Voss recalled in 1949 that none of the other internees in the witnesses wing had any news of Kammler. It seems he had completely dropped out of sight before the capitulation the year before.

Voss fully accepted the inevitability of having to undergo interrogation once more. It was part of the Allied policy that the International Military Tribunal should put German industrialists through a fine-mesh screening to determine whether they had conducted their business in accordance with the internationally accepted ground rules or whether, blinded by the anticipation of Nazi victory, they had violated international treaties that would warrant indictment. No such court had even been appointed before. It had power of life and death over those classified in advance as "major war criminals" and not directly over other persons, as laid down by a charter drafted by the four victorious powers.

Had Kammler been caught and put on trial before the International Military Tribunal at Nuremberg, he would most probably have costarred with Concentration Camp Supremo SS General Oswald Pohl and other Himmler aides, in Case 4.

The general indictment charged Pohl and his SS codefendants with "acting pursuant to a common design, conspiracy. . . to establish, maintain, operate and administer throughout Germany and other countries, concentration camps and labour camps, in which thousands of persons, including prisoners of war, German civilians and nationals of other countries, were unlawfully imprisoned, enslaved, tortured and murdered. . . to supply the labour and services of the inmates of concentration camps to various industries and enterprises in Germany and other countries."

As Kammler eluded the dragnet for top Nazis and SS leaders, the IMT could only try two much lesser Himmler aides along with Pohl. SS Generals August Frank and Georg Loerner, department heads in the SS empire, were technically ex officio deputies to Pohl, but Kammler had long since eclipsed them in the SS pecking order where he ranked number three after Himmler. The Soviet judges at Nuremberg could also have insisted on trying Kammler for the decimation order he issued in 1944 of upwards of 100 forced laborers.

Pohl was hanged on June 7, 1951.

Voss recalled later, in 1949, that he had great *angst* ("fear") at the time. He was afraid his multiple involvement in the German, Austrian, and Italian arms industry, his designation as a *Wehrwirtschaftsführer* ("War Economy Leader") and his rank as *SS Sturmbannführer* in the general SS—classified as a criminal organization—would land him in the dock. By the time he had completed the first of seven extended interrogations, starting in December 1946, Goering had committed suicide, Generals Keitel and Jodl had been executed, and Speer and Neurath were awaiting their transfer to the four-power Spandau prison in West Berlin to serve their sentences. They left for Berlin in July 1947, handcuffed.[2]

The American interrogators attached to the office of the chief U.S. counsel, Brigadier General Telford Taylor, were economic policy specialists. Their interest as far as Voss was concerned was primarily to probe his role and Skoda's role in the Third Reich arms-production program. Voss's inside knowledge of Skoda, the international arms trade, its leaders, as well as its worldwide interlocking links, presented a special dilemma for U.S. interrogators. The aspect that worried them most was that Voss was able to bring into focus Skoda's and his own very close private prewar ties with the armament industries of the four Allies.

This factor presented a likelihood that discussion of Voss's evidence might stray into areas politically embarrassing for all four victorious Allies. Their concern stemmed from a warning signal from U.S. Justice Robert H. Jackson, the prominent jurist the United States had picked to represent it on the bench at Nuremberg. Mindful that the defense had been given access to captured German Foreign Office records, which otherwise might not have seen daylight for thirty years, Jackson was quick to realize that a formula was needed to keep the trial on a level that would not "brazenly invite accusations" on the principle of *tu quoque*, suggesting that the Allies had taken equally serious actions.[3]

To avoid a possible charge that an attempt was being made to influence impartial judges to exclude politically inconvenient topics, Justice Jackson suggested that the prosecution should adhere to Article 18 of the United Nations Charter on war crimes, specifically that hearings should be confined to "issues raised" and rule out irrelevant issues and "statements of any kind whatsoever." In evident implementation of these guidelines, Voss noted that some specific witnesses he expected to document close prewar ties between Skoda and the United States and Berlin were *not* called—even though their names and the key positions they had held were known to the prosecution—until the defense identified them.

In the Wilhelmstrasse (Foreign Office) case, in which Voss testified for the defense, an American witness refused to appear in person in the case of a close business associate, Paul Pleiger, head of the Reich's steel, coal, and mining enterprises, but submitted an affidavit describing Pleiger as an "arrogant Nazi." Documents presented by the defense not only showed that the two were on a first-name basis, but that the American executive was in the habit of signing even personal Christmas greetings "Heil Hitler." The American witness was Herman A. Brassart, head of a New York firm of consulting engineers that had built the Skoda affiliate, Salzgitter Iron Ore and Metallurgical Works, also part of "Hermann Goering Reich Works."

Another potential witness, in a position to document the very close prewar ties between Skoda and the British government, was likewise not called. He was A. Outrata, general manager of the Skoda affiliate, Brünner Waffenwerke, which designed and built the Bren rapid-firing machine gun for the British Army and set up production facilities in Britain just before the outbreak of the war in 1939. That June, 1939, on the pretext that his wife needed specialist treatment in England, Outrata took her to London, but did not return to Czechoslovakia until 1945, to serve as economics minister for the first provisional government of Czechoslovakia in Prague.

In the course of the interrogations, Voss unfolded the desperate efforts to which Hitler, Goering, Speer, and Goebbels resorted, in order to conceal the true facts of the crumbling Reich economy from the public. Speer alone was forthright enough to warn Hitler that the tremendous Allied superiority in equipment "cannot be made up by bravery."[4]

The American interrogators treated Voss with deference. He was never indicted and was released to his Bavarian home upon conclusion of his interrogation sessions. Expecting to be able to slam the door on the war and concentrate on finding a job, Voss was soon jarred out of his projected program by a new call from the U.S. government in 1948.

This time he was asked to provide background on Skoda's military and research operations for U.S. counterintelligence. This meant a series of interrogations at the U.S. European Command Counterintelligence Center at Camp King Oberursel, near Frankfurt.[5] Because of the changed political situation and realization that the Soviet Union posed a major military threat to the United States and its allies, American intelligence officers at Oberursel concentrated on seeking details of Skoda's military production, the type and fields of research it was engaged in, and its development operations.

As all German state funds for the various research and development operations, including those for the Waffen SS, had been channeled through Voss, he was in a position to provide very full background material. Voss recalled that the American intelligence officers were also interested in the names and the specialist fields of the Skoda and Brünner Waffenwerke designers and engineers who had accepted contracts to go to the Soviet Union in 1945.

Interrogation proceeded smoothly until Voss brought up the undercover SS research think tank operation he and Kammler had set up at Skoda. He mentioned that through the default of an American officer on the detachment in charge of the Skoda plant in May 1945, the cream of the advance research material (including work on second generation secret weapons and the application of nuclear energy to aircraft and missile production) had slipped into Soviet hands, despite his all-out effort to prevent the hemorrhage. The disclosure hit the intelligence officers like a bombshell. The leakage had evidently been withheld from them by Washington.

From then on, interrogation sessions were attended by a senior officer on the staff of U.S. Military Governor Lieutenant General Lucius D. Clay, Voss recalled. Voss was then specifically warned that the subject matter of the loss of the SS think tank secrets to the Soviets was classified and must remain so.

By late 1949 Voss was finally through with his interrogation sessions. He found it more and more difficult to pinpoint a new field of activity. By then he was fifty-three. Dismantling was still in full swing. Political resentment against Germany, failure of the Allies to agree on how German industry could be used to help reconstruct Europe was compounded by the tactics of some of Germany's European neighbors, anxious to eliminate or block German economic competition for as long as possible.

American industrial leaders were the first to realize that a delay in German recovery would continue to keep American taxes high, since the United States was spending "billions to keep alive millions of Germans." U.S. High Commissioner John J. McCloy's blunt appeal in October 1949— "Let's stop this senseless dismantling"—caused a furor in Washington, London, Paris, and Moscow.[6]

In 1951, with the rupture of British-Egyptian relations and the ending of Britain's exclusive role as Egypt's military adviser and principal supplier of military equipment, the already explosive Middle East situation suddenly worsened. As the United States stepped into the vacuum in its role as the policeman of the world, it found that King Farouk's position was untenable. Secret talks were then opened with Colonel Gamel Abdul Nasser, a rising member of the powerful Free Officers Committee.

Nasser reached out to the CIA to help build up an independent Egyptian armament industry and establish military intelligence and secret services. There was also urgent need for military advisers, to help train the Egyptian Army.

Above all, there was need for someone to coordinate the vast web.

Officially the CIA could not figure in such a deal, so the CIA director, Allen Dulles, asked German intelligence chief General Rheinhold Gehlen, former head of Hitler's East European intelligence, for help. Voss was the man Egypt chose. He was immediately appointed chief of the military central planning board. He was to work with the War Ministry. At the invitation of General Muhammed Naguib, later president and premier, Voss flew to Cairo aboard an Egyptian military aircraft Naguib sent to Switzerland for him. At the time Voss did not have the necessary papers to make the trip overtly.

After the conclusion of negotiations, fully backed by the personal approval of Chancellor Konrad Adenauer, Voss, his staff, and their families were provided with documents certifying that their mission was in the "urgent economic interest" of the Federal Republic of Germany. Soon the Cairo operation was in full swing.[7] For Voss it was as if someone had suddenly turned the clock back to his Skoda days. He lost no time reaching out for a team of German experts to train the Egyptian Army, to build guided missiles, supersonic aircraft, and tanks. A number of former senior officers of the Wehrmacht were given contracts, as were top-caliber aircraft and tank designers. Later three top Skoda experts joined the Cairo team. Voss was in his element. News of his appointment rated banner headlines on both sides of the Atlantic and throughout the Arab world. German communities in Latin America were jubilant. A screaming lead story in the *London Daily Mail* in February 1952 proclaimed that "the man who made cannons for Hitler now heads an unofficial German Military Mission to Cairo. It includes one of Field Marshal Erwin Rommel's Corps Commanders in Normandy."

The general who made Britain's hackles rise was retired

Panzer General Wilhelm Fahrmbacher. Some days later the *Daily Mail* wrote: "Britain regards presence of ex-Rommel Generals in Cairo a serious matter." Questions were asked in Parliament. To calm public anger, the Foreign Office announced that the Cairo reports were "not official."

Voss's group of technical experts at one time rose to some 200. It included Professor Eugene Sänger, world renowned rocket authority for his "skip flight" theory, Professor Kurt Tank, whose Condor was the first passenger aircraft to cross the Atlantic nonstop, and who designed the Focke-Wulf 190 fighter. His plans for the TA-183 fell into Soviet hands and are thought to have formed the basis of the Soviet MIG-15. Last but not least, Professor Kurt Messerschmitt, whose ME-262 was the world's first jet fighter, acted as an outside consultant.

The very close official and personal relations Voss had maintained with Chancellor Adenauer, Secretary of State Walter Hallstein, the Defense Ministry, and leading Cabinet ministers, made Voss the embryo German Federal Republic's first major political hot potato. It came about when German ambassador to Egypt, Guenther Pawelka, asked for his retirement, angered over the fact that Bonn was dealing with Voss directly, instead of through the German embassy in Cairo. It was said that leading officials in the Bonn Foreign Office consulted Voss directly in all matters affecting German-Egyptian relations.

More fat was thrown on the fire when the *London Daily Express* came up with a twin salvo. First, it disclosed that Bonn was using the prestige of the Voss mission to launch a major investment and economic drive into the Arab world. Then it went on to claim that the drive was being coordinated by Hitler's financial wizard Dr. Hjalmar Schacht, former president of the Reichsbank.[8] Acquitted of all charges at Nuremberg, he was then head of his own bank in Düsseldorf, the money capital of the steel and coal-rich Ruhr.

*   *   *

In June 1953, Naguib toppled ex-King Farouk's baby son, declared Egypt a republic, and assumed the presidency and the premiership. The situation radically changed once more, when Nasser deposed Naguib in November 1954, suppressed the Communist party, and jailed its leaders. Paradoxically, this did not deter him from ordering arms from Skoda, already part of the Soviet sphere of influence.

The U.S. government had been pouring millions of dollars into Egypt to bolster its economy. Then it reportedly sent three million dollars through the CIA instructing it to pay the money over to Nasser. Some Egyptian media suggested that the funds had in fact been intended for Naguib.

The rapid fluctuation of political events in Egypt and its potential impact on the rest of the Middle East began to worry Voss and several of his associates. He foresaw the first step toward a total eclipse of the German advisory group and a shift of emphasis to Soviet military advisers. His hunch proved accurate. In 1955, he drew the consequences and quit Egypt. This did not mean that he had any intention of leading a life of idleness at his villa near Munich. He had just turned sixty. His name was back in the news, and once again a household word in international armament circles.

His reluctance to remain on in Cairo once the Soviet advisers began to move in was a plus mark for him in Bonn, where the doors of Adenauer's first-floor office suite in the Palais Schaumburg Chancellory continued to remain as open to him as ever before. While in Cairo, he had a standing invitation to "drop by" at the Chancellory and Defense Ministry, whenever he was on a visit to Germany.

Though he continued to be at the disposal of the Egyptian government—he told newsmen on his return—it was an open secret that he was in the market for similar high-level consultancy work. Never having been indicted for war crimes, his Third Reich slate was clean. As a former president of Skoda and some ten other heavy industry and armament-linked enterprises he had firsthand knowledge of the Soviet heavy industry gained in several visits for Skoda up to 1941, when Hitler invaded the Soviet Union. Voss's track record of expertise was hard to beat, perhaps even unmatched, in his field.

It was this element of his stock in trade, coupled with his facility of doing all things well, automatically, that was to catapult his name into the crossroads of international politics and the rarefied world of the global armament industry in the late fifties. It was sparked by rumors, picked up by British and U.S. intelligence observers (keeping an eye on the newly created Federal Republic of Germany), that Voss was about to or had already undertaken a hush-hush, top-secret mission to Peking, either for Bonn or in response to Peking initiative.

At the time, more and more countries began to recognize the People's Republic of China, even though the United States refused to go along with Britain and the rest. The full complexities of the rumored mission deserve elaboration because of the still unsolved mystery of whether Voss, who in 1945 risked his life to prevent the nest egg of vital-to-the-West Nazi military research secrets from falling into Soviet hands, then six years later helped trailblaze Bonn's subsequent massive economic and heavy industry presence in the Arab world and Iran, should also be credited with having taken a leading role in opening the vast Chinese market for West German heavy industry and rapidly growing armament potential.

In the mid-1950s, China was in a state of flux. Peking-Moscow relations, established under a thirty-year treaty of friendship signed soon after the People's Republic was proclaimed in 1949, were far from harmonious. A growing deterioration in these relations suggested that a switch in the China-Soviet alliance was in the cards, and the limited Soviet technical assistance was not forever.[9]

It stood to reason that China would soon want to prove the feasibility of building up an independent heavy industry with a built-in armament manufacturing potential, and that it needed advice from the West. The newly created West Germany was an obvious choice. And there was no doubt that Voss was ideally suited for the job.

The scene for Bonn-Peking cooperation had already been set by Adenauer's concurrent and much publicized interest in China, adding fuel to the speculation that the rumored Voss mission may indeed have been indirectly sparked by the Chancellor. Adenauer's interest in China, far removed from his twin pet subjects of European integration and strong Bonn-Washington ties, stemmed from a startling, totally novel political analysis of the limitations of Soviet power and Moscow-Peking relations. Published in book form in West Germany in 1954, it soon became internationally quoted column material.[10]

Titled *My Six Years with Russia's Political Prisoners*, it was written by a noted physician who had never before been known to be concerned with politics. He was Dr. Wilhelm Starlinger, a German medical doctor who had spent six years in various Soviet concentration camps for "knowing too much" about the bloody Soviet rule in his hometown Königsberg, East Prussia's capital city, which came under Soviet rule in 1945. Dr. Starlinger was arrested in 1947 and released in 1954.

Sharing captivity with former top-echelon Soviet officials, Communist party central committee members, generals and intellectuals, Dr. Starlinger, as their physician, won their confidence and obtained their honest views. With their fate sealed, they no longer had anything to gain by holding back. On the basis of these talks and his personal observations, he published his notes soon after his release, one year after Stalin's death.

The Starlinger alert was keynoted by the bold and sensational prediction that sooner or later the United States would come to some sort of working relations with Red China, that as China's interest increasingly clashed with those of the Soviets, a new balance of world power would shape up in which China would detach itself from the Soviet Union and switch to cooperation with the United States and the West. The forecast made the point that the whole pattern absolutely hinged on U.S. relations with China, and that coming to terms with Peking would reopen doors for the United States and its allies, including West Germany, in the world's greatest consumer market.

The book left such a deep impression on Adenauer that he immediately brought it to the attention of U.S. Secretary of State John Foster Dulles, long before the English version first saw daylight in the United States in late November 1955. According to *Chicago Sun-Times* Bonn correspondent Frederick Kuh, writing in 1955, "Starlinger, through Adenauer, has also been influencing U.S. policy." As of the mid-1950s, Bonn had already maintained economic relations with People's China, but official recognition did not come until 1973, one year after U.S. President Richard M. Nixon's historic visit.

There is no *official* confirmation nor records that a Voss mission to China did in fact take place. Because of Bonn's close relations with the United States, which at that time had not yet recognized the People's Republic, Adenauer could not in any case be overtly associated with the mission. The fact that it involved a top Third Reich armament and heavy industry leader, whose postwar emergence as head of Egypt's Central Military Planning Board, had only recently generated angry headlines in London, Washington, Moscow, Paris, and elsewhere.

By the nature of such a mission all agencies involved would automatically have invoked maximum secrecy, to the point of disinformation where need be. A British diplomat with several years of Chinese experience recalled that a foreign VIP whose presence the host country did not want to publicize would not even have contact with the resident community of his own country, nor, obviously, with the Peking press corps. The informant added that, in similar circumstances, China sometimes slipped key visitors in and out of China through nearby Macao, the Portuguese enclave, only a short speedboat ride from Hong Kong.

Ironically, the Egyptian government had resorted to just such tactics in 1951, when it first asked Voss to fly in for an exploratory interview. At the time, Voss did not have an exit permit, nor was his passport endorsed for the trip. So he had to make his way to Switzerland for his rendezvous with an Egyptian official and thence was flown to and from Cairo on an Egyptian military aircraft, not subject to immigration and passport control.

Equally mystery-shrouded is the alleged hush-hush China visit in the mid-1960s of top German V-2 rocket expert Professor Dr. Wolfgang Pilz, formerly at Peenemunde on the staff of Dr. Wernher von Braun. As did Voss, Dr. Pilz put in a postwar stint in Cairo, heading a German team of experts, helping Nasser to construct "homegrown" rockets, such as the Conqueror. On a similar assignment, he is believed to have designed the French Veronique rocket. Dr. Pilz hurriedly left the Cairo project in 1965 after a number of threats on his life. A letter bomb, addressed to him, blinded his secretary. From then on he carefully covered his movements, to the point where he was even out of touch with his solicitor, his counsel recalled recently. There was talk that the threats came from Israeli pressure groups. His rumored China mission was said to have taken place subsequently.

By the early eighties, in the wake of U.S. recognition in 1978, China's Western-assisted military modernization program was in full swing. The frequent presence in Chinese ports of modern U.S. and other NATO warships with their sophisticated, advanced equipment and high-powered, expert sales team aboard was no news, wrote Rainer W. Rupp of NATO's Economic Directorate in his February 1981 review, titled "China's Strategic Aims and Military Modernization" (*NATO Review*, February 1981).

After his Cairo assignment Voss devoted much of his time to consultancy work and writing on foreign policy issues. A paper he wrote in 1972 urged the Bonn government to seek closer political and economic ties with Czechoslovakia, in effect laying the groundwork for the subsequent Bonn-Prague normalization treaty of 1974.

Voss died the same year, aged seventy-eight. Ironically, he received his death sentence from his own doctor. According to a close friend who negotiated the original door-opening for Voss with the Cairo government, the doctor warned him some time before, "You have bone cancer. You must stop playing golf. If you don't, you will just collapse on the green without any warning and drop dead."

Voss's death in 1974 came almost exactly five years before his dramatic 1945 eyewitness account of the hemorrhage of SS think tank research secrets to the Soviets would routinely be due for declassification under the provisions of the U.S. Freedom of Information Act.

He could not have known that the normal thirty-year rule permitting the release of secret World War II material and reports would be suspended in respect to the classified part of the complex of information he had provided. He had given it first to U.S. authorities in Pilsen in 1945, then at Nuremberg, and finally to U.S. intelligence at the European Command Counterintelligence Center at Camp King, Oberursel, near Frankfurt Main, in 1949. The files continued to be suppressed and remain under lock and key in Washington, well beyond the thirty-year rule. The motive for this remains a four-decade mystery.

Equally mysterious is the fact that although Voss attempted to broach the subject of Kammler's disappearance and to stress the importance of locating him, if he survived, U.S. intelligence—a clan never at a loss to defend its own turf—sidestepped the issue. This point was recently recalled by Voss's lawyer, Franz von Papen, Jr.[11], who acted for Voss between 1946 and 1949.

TWELVE

EPILOGUE

> We seek him here, we seek him
> there,
> Those Frenchies seek him every-
> where.
> Is he in Heaven? Is he in Hell?
> That *demmed* elusive Pimpernel.
> BARONESS EMMUSKA ORCZY, *The
> Scarlet Pimpernel*

THE ALL-OUT HUNT TO catch the elusive Scarlet Pimpernel, the eighteenth-century hero of fiction and screen who flitted between England and revolutionary France with the greatest of ease in various disguises, was not repeated at the close of World War II. No one seems to have mounted a search for Nazi Germany's equally elusive "Rocket Czar," SS General Hans Kammler, when he dropped out of sight on April 17, 1945, twenty-one days before the end of the Third Reich.

A number of questions have remained unanswered. Did he go east? If so, was it prearranged? What top secrets did he take? Did he go west? Or was he buried in an unmarked grave in a remote forest between Pilsen and Prague, after taking his own life, as some of his surviving aides, who still feel hero worship for him, would have it almost four decades later?

Alternatively, did he choose to live out his days in a remote abbey, devoting his multifaceted talents to yet a new venture? Did he live to commercially market the exquisite liqueur produced at the abbey, in return for the impenetrable cover it could provide in the hour of need?

Perhaps Kammler remembered his Russian history. A similar ploy was said to have been adopted, for political reasons, by Czar Alexander I of Russia (1777–1825). According to legend, the handsome forty-eight-year-old Czar did not die in the Crimea as announced in 1825. Seeking a new life, he vanished behind the walls of a monastery at Minsk, circulating reports of his own death with the skills he had acquired in planting disinformation with Napoleon.

Hitler's Armament Minister Albert Speer, whom Kammler was groomed to replace, appears to have accepted Dornberger's suicide theory as feasible and referred to it in his last book, featuring the infiltration of the SS into the armament industry.[1]

Whatever the truth, Kammler's appearance on the postwar scene in the West would have been acutely embarrassing both for the United States and Britain. Neither could have indicted him under the catch-all count of "crimes against peace" for running the indiscriminate terror rocket bombardment of London, Paris, Antwerp, Liege, and Brussels. The same applied to Dornberger, who codeveloped and produced the V-2.

The embarrassing fact was that, by the end of 1945 when the first Nuremberg trials opened, both of Hitler's "reprisal weapons," the V-1 and V-2, had already been earmarked for inclusion in the Big Four's arsenals. They paved the way for the U.S. and Soviet land-and-sea-based Cruise missiles and the U.S. Pershing/Soviet SS series of ballistic missiles of the 1980s.

The Soviets, enriched by two "Kammler Enterprises," the

unexpected prize of a fully intact V-2 factory naively left for them on June 21 by the U.S. Army, which initially captured the site in April, and the further bonanza of the SS research think tank secrets at Pilsen on May 12, had no reason to raise the issue of Kammler's whereabouts at the Nuremberg war crime trials.[2]

Apart from brief references to his career in a crop of postwar accounts touching on the German secret weapon and jet aircraft scene, Kammler was given little attention. The various commands he had held in a surprisingly wide field of unlinked projects and programs, and his gradual emergence as one of the people Hitler and Himmler really trusted during the final two years of the Third Reich, was played down to the point where he became a "no-person." Meanwhile the stars and self-appointed lesser stars of the Nazi galaxy presented their mostly ghostwritten, idealized versions of the role they saw themselves as having played in the passing Nazi parade.

While inevitably spotlighting themselves, even those directly involved with Kammler casually cut his role and tremendous influence to the bone, wherever and whenever possible. Significantly, none of the newly fledged autobiographies deemed it worthwhile to include a shot of Kammler in their usually well-illustrated and documented books—not even Speer nor the Peenemunde luminaries von Braun and Dornberger, by then well rooted in the United States.

Nonetheless, in 1948, the all-but-forgotten Kammler complex had received an unexpected but strictly unpublicized boost when Washington—undoubtedly prompted by the new strategic considerations arising from the Cold War—decided to take a new look at the arms-making potential the Soviets had acquired with Skoda. It was logical that the expertise of former Skoda president Wilhelm Voss would be sought, especially in view of his recent valuable testimony as a witness at Nuremberg, on the role Skoda played in the Third Reich economy. Voss also had given a detailed assessment of Skoda's likely role as an arms maker for the Soviet armament industry.

The U.S. interrogators also showed interest in the areas where the lost research secrets would most likely give the Soviets a head start in key military research. It was at this point that Voss touched on the Kammler Group's work in applying nuclear energy for missile and aircraft propulsion.

Voss could not possibly have known, and the American intelligence officers obviously did not tell him, that even while the Frankfurt interrogations were taking place, a group of American nuclear experts, commissioned by the Atomic Energy Commission (AEC) were probing the same complex under a cloak of maximum security.[3] The mini-nuclear cell, fitted to some sophisticated modern-day U.S. and Soviet satellites, to provide on-board power for the radar and other equipment, is a spinoff of research conducted in this field.

The hush-hush program was codenamed NEPA (Nuclear Energy Propulsion Aircraft), and was popularly referred to as the Lexington Project. It had been set up with a multimillion-dollar budget in the light of newly available intelligence reports on the wartime work done by German scientists at Skoda, the Junkers Aircraft factory at Dessau, and by other groups. It was also fueled by the reported postwar Soviet progress in the field of nuclear propulsion for missiles and aircraft. The project was headed by Walter G. Whitman, head of the Department of Chemistry at the Massachusetts Institute of Technology. Its recommendations were subsequently summarized in the Lexington Report, but were never published.

Because of its possible relevance to the Kammler-Voss-Skoda story and the lapse of more than thirty years, I put in a formal request with the National Archives in 1979 for the release, to me, of the Lexington Report, under the Freedom of Information Act.

My quest met with the same runaround and stonewalling I had faced in attempting to obtain the release of the Voss interrogation reports of 1948/1949. The coverup climaxed with the categoric statement by the Department of the Army that there are "no records identifiable" with Voss.

Although in face of the evidence there could be no denial of the existence of the Lexington Report, no trace of it could be found. My query resulted in a wild-goose chase and referral from department to department: Army, Navy, Air Force, National Archives, Department of Energy, and MIT, to mention just a few. Each professed ignorance as to the report's whereabouts.

MIT came up with the classic excuse: Dr. Whitman, who was director of the project, is no longer living and, although he was an MIT professor, his papers are not in the Institute Archives. The fact that Washington has continued to suppress both the Voss interrogation reports and the indirectly linked Lexington Report will not surprise historians and journalists familiar with the uphill task of searching for prime source material.

For the record, a very similar coverup has been maintained since 1945 in regard to the *Van Vliet Report*. It is the eyewitness account of West Pointer U.S. Army Colonel John H. Van Vliet, Jr. on his inspection of the mass graves of Polish officers in the Katyn Forest, near Smolensk, Russia, when he was a prisoner of war of the Germans during World War II. His report was made upon repatriation from Nazi captivity in 1945. In it he expressed his firm conviction, from on-the-spot evidence, that the Polish officers had been massacred by the Russians, and not, as the Soviets claimed, the Nazis.

His report was ignored at the time as politically embarrassing and later officially declared as missing, according to the official record of U.S. Congressional Hearing in 1952,[4] a part of which I covered. The Van Vliet eyewitness account of his visit to the Katyn Forest has never, to this day, been found.

The coverup recalls a similar smokescreen laid down by the U.S. Army in Germany in 1947 after I first broke the story of the disappearance of the captured German National Bank (Reichsbank) gold, foreign currency, and precious metal reserves from the custody of U.S. Army and civilian personnel. The crime was subsequently listed by the Guinness Book of Records as the "Greatest Robbery in History." The full scandal could not be probed at the time. It took British authors Ian Sayer and Douglas Botting nine years' research to present the full dossier (*Nazi Gold*, Granada, with the *Sunday Times*, London, 1984).

The authors of *Nazi Gold* wrote that they had found clear indication that relevant official documents had been destroyed by the U.S. Army.

"Elephants are seldom lost," as a London schoolgirl once remarked in a test paper on the species,[5] but documents on multimillion dollar projects and other complexes that concern matters that are militarily or politically sensitive can, apparently, vanish completely from the U.S. National Archives.

LIST OF APPENDICES

1. Nazi-Soviet military cooperation during two world wars

2. SHAEF intelligence summary of March 1945

3. Alfried Krupp, serving a twelve-year sentence for aiding the preparation of World War II and other war crimes, is asked by Allies in 1950 to make arms for the United States, then involved in the Korean conflict. Since 1938, Krupp has had a controlling interest in Skoda.

4. U.S. aviator Colonel Charles A. Lindbergh's visit to the Nordhausen underground aircraft and missile factory on an official U.S. mission in June 1945, before the site was handed over to the Soviets.

5. Brigadier General Truman Boudinot's Combat Command B. U.S. Third Army, liberates British prisoners of war at a German camp. Some Britons were captured in Normandy.

6. Background on Soviet master spy, Dr. Richard Sorge, German journalist, who used German embassy in Tokyo as his base.

7. Achievements of German scientists have survived on *both* sides of the Iron Curtain in one spin-off project or another.

Appendix 1

Military cooperation between Russia and Germany dates back to the eighteeenth century. In 1923 Russia helped Germany circumvent the Versailles Treaty and its arms limitations. Cooperation over the years ranged from setting up clandestine aircraft production in Russia (Junkers) to training facilities for German officers in handling tanks and large armies, forbidden under the treaty. The close contacts continued between the two wars, resulting in friendship between the general staffs of the two countries.

By the time Hitler came to power in 1933, all was ready for him. In a reverse facility, Red Army officers now attended at German staff courses, while German technicians and Air Force officers, including Hitler's air adjutant, Colonel Nicholas von Below, received flight training in Russia.

Though many of the Red Army officers known to be close to their German opposite numbers were purged by Stalin in 1937, contacts continued until Germany invaded Russia in 1941. In some cases contacts continued beyond 1941. Churchill was aware of this and made use of the information, planting stories he wanted to percolate to Berlin in Moscow.

Appendix 2

The SHAEF Intelligence Summary of March 11, 1945 stated in part:

The main trend of German defence policy does seem directed primarily to the safeguarding of the Alpine zone. . . this area is by the very nature of the terrain practically impenetrable. The evidence indicates that considerable numbers of SS and specially chosen units are being withdrawn to Austria, that some of the most important ministries and personalities of the Nazi Regime are already established in the Redoubt area. . . defended both by nature and the most efficient secret weapons yet invented. The powers that have hitherto guided Germany will survive to reorganize her resurrection, their armaments will be manufactured in bomb-proof factories, food and equipment will be stored in vast underground caverns, and specially selected corps of young men will be trained in guerilla warfare, so that a whole underground Army can be fitted out. . . to liberate Germany from the occupying powers.

Appendix 3

In October 1950, four months after Soviet-assisted North Korean troops invaded South Korea, the United States, British, and French governments appealed to Alfried Krupp to help provide arms for the U.S. engagement in Korea. Krupp was still serving a twelve-year sentence for aiding the war effort, exploiting slave labor, and other war crimes.

In a parallel move, the Allies also turned to Chancellor Konrad Adenauer, asking him to help provide a military contribution to the European Defense Community (EDC), later NATO.

The Western Allies soon tore up Germany's eleven-million-tons-a-year steel limit and urged the steel barons to go all out in the fight against Communism.

In November, Krupp, still a convict, called his first board meeting since the fall of the Third Reich and summoned his directors to Landsberg Prison, where Hitler had written *Mein Kampf.* The same month, holding one of the highest security clearances of any convict in penal history, Krupp was informed of Washington's determination to see a new German sword forged. The Federal Republic was to provide a contingent for NATO.

Krupp's clemency followed. He was freed on February 3, 1951.

At the 1961 Essen celebrations of the firm's 150th anniversary, former West German Federal President Theodore Heuss said that "malicious clichés," sparked by the hatred of war, had created a "false and outrageous image of *Die Firma* ("The Firm") as an 'Annex to Hell,' " while Skoda, Britain's Vickers Armstrong, the U.S. Bethlehem Steel, and France's Schneider Creusot were depicted as *Himmlische Engel* ("Heavenly Angels").

Appendix 4

Colonel Lindbergh, in his *Wartime Diary*, also describes in equally horrific detail the scenes he encountered on entering the Dora concentration and extermination camp, which provided some of the labor for the Nordhausen plant. His horror at "Man's Inhumanity to Man" was enhanced by recollections of equally appalling scenes he had witnessed during his recent tour of duty in the Pacific. But the perpetrators there were his own compatriots. The victims were the Japanese.

Appendix 5

After leaving Nordhausen in charge of the U.S. Third Army elements, Combat Command B liberated the Eisleben British prisoner-of-war camp on April 12, on its way toward Dessau. Eisleben is the birthplace of Martin Luther (1483–1546). It had been a long wait for the 430 Britons, some of whom had been prisoners since the debacle of Dunkirk, the Norwegian campaign, Africa, and Crete.

The CCB diarist wrote: "It was a great day for the erstwhile prisoners. Traditionally reserved English officers and enlisted men broke down and cheered as the battle group formations thundered through town. A British airborne infantry major summed it up. "We knew you were coming when that first Sherman tank rolled over the hill. I was so happy, I cried."

Appendix 6

Sorge's name and that of Ozaki Hozumi, his principal assistant, executed with him in Tokyo in 1944, repeatedly came up during the post-war investigation of Washington's China policy when it switched from supporting the Nationalist Chiang Kai-shek to Chou en-Lai's Communist regime. Hozumi, a prominent journalist and adviser to the Konoye Cabinet, was a frequent contributor to the U.S. Institute of Pacific Relations publications. Hozumi first joined forces with Sorge in Shanghai.

In his memoirs written shortly before his execution, Sorge paid tribute to American writer and China expert Agnes Smedley for facilitating his work in Shanghai by making her house available for KGB meetings. The 25,000-word U.S. Military Government report on Sorge ("The Sorge Spy Ring: A Case History of International Espionage in the Far East," prepared by G-2 of U.S. Military Government for Japan) describes Smedley as an "American Soviet spy" and one of the "early perpetrators of the hoax that the Chinese Communists were not really Communists but only local agrarian revolutionaries."

Incredibly, Sorge's German friends and employers did not seem to bother about the fact that he was Russian born and that his grandfather, Adolf Sorge, had served as secretary to Karl Marx. As an accredited Far East correspondent for prestigious German newspapers, Sorge was even provided with an office at the German Embassy in Tokyo, and finally became member of German intelligence as well. Agnes Smedley died in 1950 and is buried in Peking. Sorge's services to the KGB were not forgotten. In 1981, it raised a statue for him at his birthplace, Baku, in southern Russia. East Germany featured him on a stamp. A Western film on Sorge was shown throughout the Soviet Union, and currently he is popularized in a James Bond-type Soviet adventure series, portraying a glamorous KGB agent. The series is by a former Soviet foreign correspondent in Bonn.

In the light of the prominent positions Voss held in the Third Reich Establishment, the evasive official U.S. response to my 1980 Freedom of Information request to National Archives for transcripts of Voss's Interrogations between 1946 and 1949, borders on the absurd. The Army Intelligence and Security Command's claim that it had "no records" identifiable with the Wilhelm Voss referred to in the FOI request was utterly exploded by the discovery, in 1982, of a duplicate (alas incomplete) set of transcripts at the British Imperial War Museum Archives in London, where the documents had landed 36 years before under an exchange-of-information arrangement.

DEPARTMENT OF THE ARMY
US ARMY INTELLIGENCE AND SECURITY COMMAND
FORT GEORGE G. MEADE, MARYLAND 20755

IACSF-FI   1 May 1980

Mr. Tom Agoston

Dear Mr. Agoston:

This is in response to your letter of 14 April 1980, to this office,
requesting under the provisions of the Freedom of Information Act 5
USC552, records concerning   Wilhelm Voss,
This correspondence was received in this office on 22 April 1980.

We have conducted a survey of the automated Defense Central Index of
Investigations (DCII) and the Investigative Records Repository to determine the existence of any intelligence investigative records generated
by the US Army or maintained by any other investigative agency within
the Department of Defense which would be responsive to your request.

In regard to Wilhelm Voss, we have records on several persons with this
name. To determine which records pertain to your William Voss and to
facilitate search for information responsive to your request, it will
aid us if you would provide additional information on your William Voss,
specifically, his date and place of birth. We will then be able to
determine whether or not records available at this Command would be
responsive to your request.

DEPARTMENT OF THE ARMY
US ARMY INTELLIGENCE AND SECURITY COMMAND
FORT GEORGE G. MEADE, MARYLAND 20755

IACSF-FI   19 June 1980
Mr. Tom Agoston

Dear Mr. Agoston:

This is in response to your letter of 4 June 1980 to this office requesting
records concerning   Wilhelm Voss,
provisions of the Freedom of Information Act 5 USC552. This correspondence
was received in this office on 12 June 1980.

To determine the existence of Army intelligence investigative records
concerning Wilhelm Voss, a survey was made of the Master Name Index of
the Defense Central Index of Investigations. This Index is managed by
the Defense Investigative Service for the Department of Defense. The
index is keyed to the individual's name, date and place of birth,
social security account number and service number (if any), and yields
information about the existence of investigative files concerning the
subject. We queried this index using Voss' name, and date and place of
birth. As a result of this survey, we have determined there are no Army
intelligence investigative records identifiable with him.

DEPARTMENT OF THE ARMY
US ARMY INTELLIGENCE AND SECURITY COMMAND
FORT GEORGE G. MEADE, MARYLAND 20755

IACSF-FI   5 August 1980

Mr. Tom Agoston
Dear Mr. Agoston:

This is in response to your letter of 19 July 1980 to this office requesting
records concerning   Dr. Wilhelm Voss under the provisions
of the Freedom of Information Act 5 USC552. This correspondence was
received in this office on 29 July 1980.

With regard to Dr. Wilhelm Voss, a screening of the records concerning
persons with this name, revealed no individuals identifiable with the
Wilhelm Voss described in your letter.

Appendix 7

Though Nazi military supremacy was robustly smashed during World War II, the achievements of German scientists have survived on *both* sides of the Iron Curtain in one spin-off project or another.

It took ten years or more before the world began to realize that the German "back room boys" did very much more than they were generally given credit for. This was conceded by the various experts when they began to analyze whatever had surfaced of the "Nazi Nest Egg" of scientific and military research secrets. It was also realized that the Germans were very close to discovering the secrets of the atom bomb, working hard until the end, in a race to beat the United States.

The two men whom Kammler had in part superseded in commanding the secret weapons programs—Reichmarshal Hermann Goering, Air Force Commander and Air Minister, and Armament Minister Albert Speer—had obviously more inside knowledge than most Nazi leaders of the sensitive fields where the secrets were being developed, and were acutely aware of the dangerous hemorrhage of secrets to both East and West that had taken place during the final phase of the war.

When the Nuremberg trials ended, both Goering and Speer went on record with their thoughts on the dangers they envisaged the world would inevitably be facing if all the terror weapons at man's disposal were unleashed. Goering's warning, scrawled in longhand in his prison cell before his suicide, was one of the farewell notes he left. All the notes were sequestered by the U.S. Commandant of the Nuremberg War Crimes prison (Colonel Burton C. Andrus) and are still classified by the United States. A copy of an unpublished purported version of Goering's warning in my possession is very similar in content to a statement Speer made as part of his concluding remarks at Nuremberg. It was cited by his fellow prisoner Dr. Hjalmar Greely Schacht, President of the Reichbank, in his book *Account Settled* (London: Weidenfeld, 1950), originally published after Schacht's acquittal at Nuremberg.

The Speer statement read in part:

This war ended with rockets guided by remote control, with aeroplanes flying at the speed of sound, with new-type submarines, with torpedoes which automatically guide themselves to their target, with Atom Bombs and with the prospect of terrible Chemical Warfare.

The next war will inevitably be waged with these new destructive weapons of human ingenuity. Within five or ten years, the development of war techniques will make it possible to fire rockets from continent to continent, with terrifying accuracy. At any time of the day or night, without warning, and without visible signs of danger, it will be possible perhaps with a crew of only ten men, to fire off a rocket flying faster than sound and fitted with an atomic warhead, and so destroy a million people in the heart of New York, in a matter of seconds. It is possible for the scientists of various countries to spread epidemics among men and animals, and to destroy harvests by insect warfare.

Select Bibliography

1. TEXT-RELATED MATERIAL

American Aviation Week, March-June, 1955

Archives Consulted

Department of the Army Intelligence and Technical Command, Fort Meade, Maryland

German National Archives *(Bundesarchiv)*, Koblenz
German National Archives *(Militärarchiv)*, Freiburg
Breisgau Historical Division, U.S. Forces, Europe
Imperial War Museum, London
Library Massachusetts Institute of Technology (MIT), Cambridge, Massachusetts, 1982
Military History Office, U.S. Mission, Berlin. The Berlin Document Center
National Archives, Washington
Naval History Center, Washington
Public Record Office, London
Research office for the Study of Nazi War Crimes, Hamburg
V Corps Historian, U.S. Forces, Europe

Atomic Shield, History of the U.S. Atomic Energy Commission (AEC), Hawlett and Duca, University of Pennsylvania, 1960

SELECT BIBLIOGRAPHY

Chronologies, U.S. Army in World War II

The Last Offensive: Götterdämmerung, Charles B McDonald, Washington 1973.

Special Studies, Chronology 30-April 1945, compiled by Mary H. Williams, the Office of the Chief of Military History, Department of the Army, Washington, 1960.

"Concentration Camps of Axis Powers in Europe," a declassified SHAEF report, London, 1943.

"Cruise Missiles Technology: U.S. and Soviet Union, from 1946," a report by Richard K. Betts for the Brookings Institution, Washington, 1982.

"Doenitz Government: The Last Days of the Third Reich" *(Die Letzten Tage des Dritten Reiches)* diary and documents, by Commander Walter Lüdde-Neurath, Adjutant to Grand Admiral Karl Doenitz, Göttingen University, 1951.

Himmler correspondence: from the captured files of SS Reichleader Heinrich Himmler. Exchange of letters with and reports of SS Gen. Dr. Ing. Hans Kammler. Archives of the Hoover Institution on War, Revolution and Peace, Stanford University, California.

"Katyn Massacre," Missing Report of Col. John Van Vliet, Jr., U.S. House of Representatives Select Committee Report on the Katyn forest Massacre during World War II. *Hearings:* Frankfurt Main, Germany, April 1952, Author's Notes, and Final Reports, Washington, December 1952.

Nuclear propulsion: for a proposed U.S. Civilian Space Programme Code-named the ORION Programme," report on the official halt on all research and development for the program. Freeman Dyson, for *The New Yorker,* Aug. 1979.

"Redoubt," OSS Political Reports on the German "National Redoubt Complex," Office of Strategic Services Analysis Branch, covering December 29 1944–May 1945.

"Soviet Theatre Nuclear Forces," a report by Stephen Mayer, for the International Institute of Strategic Studies, London 1984.

Skoda Works, Pilsen

Two British technical intelligence reports on the Skoda Works and missing microfilms, on the takeover of the plant by the Red Army in May 1945, and a second report in September 1945. Imperial War Museum Archives, London.

Official U.S. government transcripts of six in-depth interrogations of Skoda President Dr. Wilhelm Voss, while a witness at Nuremberg (U.S. National Archives having reported *no knowledge* of their existence).

Skoda Works documents from the Archives of Salzgitter AG, Skoda's Third Reich affiliate within the overall "Reich Works for Ore and Steel Enterprise Hermann Göering."

Skoda Annual Reports of 1939 and 1941. Archives of Salzgitter AG and the Hamburg Institute for Economic Research (HWWA)

Speer testimony (Reich Armament Minister Albert Speer) on effect of Allied bombing on Germany. Given to the U.S. Strategic Bombing Mission Survey in May 1945. U.S. National Archives, Microfilm, USSB Report No. 5 (refers to Gen. Kammler's key role.) In Britain, the transcript continues to be classified beyond the normal thirty-year rule, and is not expected to be made public before 2020. Any material sensitive to Britain is not referred to in the book.

SELECT BIBLIOGRAPHY

"The Boudinot Story," Story of Brigadier General Truman E.
    Boudinot, Commander of the Combat Command B of the U.S.
    3rd Armored Division, by his son. Lt. Col. Burton S. Boudi-
    not, for the U.S. Army Armor School, 1977, and the official
    unit history of CCB and its Commanding General, prepared
    by the U.S. 3rd Armored Division Historian.

U-boat 234 on a post VE Day transatlantic mission, author's notes
    and interview with the commander of the *U-234*, Captain
    Heinrich Fehler.

"Warsaw Uprising, Warschauer Aufstand 1944," a report by Hanns
    von Krannhals, Bernhard & Gräfe, Frankfurt *Main, 1962.*

General Background Reference Works

Canan, James W., *The Superwarriors*, Weybright and Talley, New York, 1975.

Chronik des Zweiten Weltkrieges, Atheneum/Droste, 1978.

Churchill, Winston S., *Triumph and Tragedy*, Houghton Mifflin, Boston, 1953.

Cookridge, E.H., *Gehlen*. Hodder & Stoughton, London, 1971.

German Army Order of Battle, Military Intelligence Division, U.S. War Department, Washington, 1944.

Goebbels, Paul Joseph, Reich Propaganda Minister, *Diaries 1942–45*, edited by Louis P. Lochner, Doubleday, New York, 1948.

—— *Diary—1945*, Hoffman & Campe, Hamburg, 1979.

Görlitz, Walter, *Der Deutsche Generalstab*, Frankfurter Hefte, 1952.

Guderian, Heinz, Field Marshall, *Kann West Europa verteidigt werden*. Combat potential of the Soviet and Allied Military Forces in the wake of World War II, by the General Staffer who masterminded the secret German rearmament in Russia, after World War I.

Goudsmit, Samuel A., *Alsos*, Investigation of Third Reich progress in nuclear research, Schumann, New York and Oxford University Press, 1947.

Hanfstaengl, Ernst. *The Missing Years*, London, 1957.

Hermann Goering Werke Industrial complex, background files, U.S. National Archives, Washington.

Howley, Frank, *Berlin Command*, Putnam, New York, 1959.

Irving, David, *The Mare's Nest*, Kimber, London, 1967.

Janssen, Gregor, *Das Ministerium Speer: Deutschland Rüstung im Krieg*, Ullstein, 1968.

Kesselring, Albert, Field Marshal, *The Making of The Luftwaffe*, Kenneth Macksey, Batsford, London 1978.

Lindbergh, Charles A., *Wartime Journals*, Harcourt, Brace, New York 1970.

Manchester, William, *Krupp*, Little, Brown, and Co., Boston, 1964.

McGovern, James. *Crossbow and Overcast*. William Morrow, New York, 1964, and Hutchinson, London, 1964.

Persico, Joseph, *Piercing of the Reich (by the OSS)*, Michael Joseph, London, 1979.

Peuschel, Harold, *Braune Biographien: Die Männer um Hitler*, Atheneum/Droste, 1978.

Poliakov, Leon, and Josef Wulf, *Das Dritte Reich und seine Diener*, Arami Verlags, GMBH, Grünewald, Berlin, 1956.

Reitsch, Hanna, *Fliegen—mein Leben*. J.F. Lehmanns Verlag, Munich, 1972, 1973 (originally *Deutscher Verlagsanstalt Stuttgart*, 1951).

Schmidt, Paul (Hitler's Interpreter), *Statist auf der Diplomatischer Bäuhne 1923–1945*, Atheneum, Bonn, 1949.

Starlinger, Wilhelm, *Gränzer der Soviet Macht (Limits of Soviet Power)*, Holzner, Würzburg, 1955.

Speer, Albert, *Inside the Third Reich*, Weidenfeld, London, 1970.

———*Sklavenstaat—Erinnerungen äuber meine Ausseranderset-zung, mit der SS, Deutsche Verlagsanstalt, Stuttgart 1981*.

———*Infiltration: The SS in German Armament*, Macmillan, New York, 1981.

———*Spandau: The Secret Diaries*, Collins, London, 1976.

———*Technic und Macht*, Bechtle, 1979.

Tolstoy, Nikolai, *Stalin's Secret War*, Jonathan Cape, London, 1981.

———*Victims of Yalta*, Hodder & Stoughton, London, 1977.

Von Below, Nicholas (Hitler's Adjutant, 1937–1945), *Armed Forces Adjutant to Hitler*. Hase und Köhler, Mainz, 1980.

von Braun, Wernher, *History of Rocketry* (with Fred Ordway III).

von Papen, Franz, *Memoirs*. Dutton, New York, 1942.

Who's Who in Nazi Germany, G-2, SHAEF, London, 1942.

War Crimes:

Trial of War Criminals—Nuremberg Military Tribunals, October 1946–April 1949, U.S. Government Printing Office, Washington, 1952.

Indictments, Nuremberg Military Tribunals, Cases 1–12. Office of U.S. Military Government, Nuremberg, 1946.

Calvocoressi, Peter, *Nuremberg*, Chatto & Windus, London, 1947.

Viscount Maugham, *War Crimes and the UN*. London, 1947.

War Crimes Trials—the U.S. in Germany, Gen. Lucius D. Clay.

Wilmot, Chester, *Struggle for Europe*, Collins, London, 1952.

Footnotes

Chapter One

1. A former Nazi intelligence bunker containing captured German war documents that comprise a virtual Who's Who of Nazi party membership and Nazi state personnel. It covers some 30 million detailed personal information entries, collated by the Nazis between 1933 and 1945. The records came into U.S. hands in 1945. Control is by the U.S. Mission, Berlin.

2. *Amtsgruppe C* ("C Division") of the SS Economic and Administrative Main Office WVHA *(Wirtschafts und Verwaltungshauptamt)*, commanded by his mentor, SS Oswald Pohl.

3. Auschwitz, near Cracow, Poland, was the biggest of Nazi death camps, where more than 4 million died. It was the archdiocese of Pope John Paul II when he served as cardinal archbishop of Cracow. He said in 1972: "It is unique for the sheer scale of its horrifying contempt for the human person, the extent to which it witnessed the destruction of one human being by another."

4. Enough to build 2,500 one-family houses, according to a German brick manufacturer.

5. Pohl was hanged on June 7, 1951 after being found guilty of war crimes, conspiracy, and crimes against humanity. The execution, covered by the author, took place at Fort Landsberg, the prison where Hitler wrote *Mein Kampf* and where Alfried Krupp served his sentence for war crimes.

Chapter Two

1. At his Nuremberg war crimes trial, Alfried Krupp's defense lawyers did their best to dispel Krupp's image as the Reich's *Kanonenkönig*

("Cannon King"). This was "just a myth and absurd." The "Wehrmacht guns were made by Skoda," the defense claimed in 1947.

2. In his book *Spandau, The Secret Diaries* (Frankfurt: Spandauer Tagebäucher, Ullstein, 1975), Albert Speer boasts that it was he who, as armaments minister, ordered German nuclear scientists to switch their research effort into building a "uranium motor" when Werner Heisenberg could not promise to complete an atom bomb in less than three to five years.

3. It was located in the Taunusstrasse, in Berlin's Grünewald district.

Chapter Three

1. According to Teutonic legend, Holy Roman Emperor Frederick I (1123–90), known in Italy as Barbarossa, is not dead but only slumbering somewhere in the Harz Mountains and will awaken one day to restore the Reich to its former glory.

2. *Berlin Command* (New York: Putnam, 1950).

3. Joseph Persico, *Piercing Through the Reich* (London: Michael Joseph, 1979).

4. General Omar Bradley, *The Soldier's Story* (New York: Holt, 1951).

5. The internationally operating Soviet espionage ring, known as the "Red Orchestra," claimed that it was so well dug in during the war, it was in a position to flash to Moscow secret Wehrmacht instructions to army commands before the addressee had received them. The German end of the spy ring was smashed by the Nazis, but other arms survived after the war in Britain and elsewhere. The late General Reinhold Gehlen, president of the Federal German Intelligence, believed that British SIS defector Kim Philby was recruited by the British arm. (*Memoirs.* Translated by David Irving. London: Collins, 1972).

6. General Omar Bradley, *The Soldier's Story* (New York: Holt, 1951).

7. *Saturday Evening Post* (August 2, 1952).

8. Stephen E. Ambrose, *Eisenhower* (New York: Simon and Schuster, 1983), p. 403.

9. U.S. Republican publicists, trying to whitewash Eisenhower's record from the day he declared himself ready to accept nomination for the presidency, never fully succeeded in expunging the black mark.

In 1952, when his acceptance for the nomination was a foregone conclusion, Eisenhower, then NATO commander, granted the author an interview on European defense issues. Prior to the interview, the general's aide requested the author not to raise issues relating to World War II.

10. Bradley Smith, *Shadow Warriors and the Origins of the CIA* (New York: Basic Books, 1983).

11. In 1968, within a period of thirteen days in October, six top German officers and officials took their lives in Bonn and at intelligence headquarters at Pullach, near Munich. One, Admiral Hermann Luedke, was under investigation over alleged espionage activities. He was chief of NATO logistics, with knowledge of the location of 16,000 tactical nuclear warheads for possible use against the Soviets. Another officer, wartime Major General Horst Wendland, had been tipped as likely future head of the Federal Intelligence Service (Bundesnachrichtendienst, BND), founded and initially headed by the legendary General Reinhold Gehlen, Wendland's wartime commanding officer. The Bonn government stated at the time that "none of the mass suicides" other than Admiral Luedke's involved "security matters."

12. General Boudinot, a veteran of World War I, commanded the first Allied troops to enter Germany in force during World War II, and the first to occupy and capture a German town (Roetgen, on September 12, 1944), the first invading troops to take a German town since Napoleonic days, his unit historian wrote. Today, Boudinot Hall, housing the command and staff department of the U.S. Army Armor School, Fort Knox, Kentucky, commemorates the general's role in the development of modern mobile warfare.

13. Colonel Toftoy, later major general, subsequently commanded the Redstone Arsenal at Huntsville, Alabama, where von Braun and his group of 120 Peenemunde experts resumed their work on V-2s and space rockets.

14. When the Red Army arrived, it was able to resume full production at once. It still had some 2,300 technicians able to construct V-2s on the spot, though there were neither designers nor pioneers of the vision and caliber of the Peenemunde team Kammler had evacuated to Bavaria.

The one senior engineer who had chosen to remain on and who subsequently headed the Nordhausen operation for the Soviets was Helmut Goettrop, von Braun's former assistant, arrested by Himmler in 1944 for his alleged "defeatist attitude." Goettrop and his Nordhausen team were subsequently taken to the Soviet Union under a ten-year service contract. They were repatriated in 1955.

Chapter Four

1. The commanding officer of the Penang submarine base and several other members of the staff have survived the war and regularly meet at reunions of the Federation of German Submarine Crews in West Berlin.

2. According to some reports, he was en route to try a group of German businessmen alleged to have engaged in major black-market activities with rubber. Other reports said he was en route to investigate a breach of security involving the espionage activities of Soviet superspy Dr. Richard Sorge, a German journalist who tipped Moscow of the pending German invasion in 1941 and later that year the pending Japanese sneak attack on Pearl Harbor. Sorge had worked very closely with the German Ambassador, who was unaware of his undercover activities (See Appendix 6).

3. Wolfgang Hirschfeld, *Feindfahrte Vienna* (Vienna: Paul Neff, 1982).

4. It was the fear that Germany was getting dangerously close to building an atom bomb that prompted the British-Norwegian commando raid on Norsk Hydro in Norway in 1943 to block supplies of heavy water from reaching the Reich. It is incontestable that the Norsk Hydro expedition has a claim to marking a turning point in history in its preventing Hitler from making an atomic bomb. The combined operation was set up by Britain's Special Operations Executive.

5. Arthur Victor Sellwood, *The Warring Seas—Dynamite for Hire* (London: Laurie, 1956).

Chapter Five

1. The U.S. technical intelligence section, which moved into the area after the German surrender, picked Oberammergau as its headquarters for the same reason. Some of the Soviet technical intelligence officers attached to the U.S. mission likewise worked out of Oberammergau, doing their best to lure any German scientist working for the mission to Russia. Top German jet expert Helmut Schelp (formerly with Junkers) assigned as adviser to the U.S. mission, had to be provided with round-the-clock protection by a section of G.I. bodyguards, who even mounted guard outside his billet at night with an armed half-track. The story was disclosed by American aviator Colonel Charles A. Lindbergh, *Wartime Diary*, (New York: Harcourt Brace Jovanovich, 1970), then a U.S. Navy consultant on a technical aspect of wartime German aircraft and missile production. Because of its sensitive nature, publication of

the book was delayed for more than twenty-five years.

2. In the 1980s, the capacity of wind tunnels still hovers around Mach-10. But United States–German aerodynamics experts have pointed out that, as there is no major guided missile production in Europe—other than in the Soviet Union—tunnels of this capacity, geared for supersonic speeds, are concentrated in the United States.

3. Other pioneering work concentrated on a submarine-launched eighty-one-kiloton baby helicopter, to serve as a spotter aircraft.

4. The Hitler decree of March 27, 1945, appointing Kammler as jet aircraft production plenipotentiary and putting Goering and Speer under his command in this field, was tantamount to an Open-Sesame to any aircraft production plant and carried the weight of a personal order from Hitler.

5. Dornberger later wrote: "I felt like a violin maker who, after many months of work, completes the instrument and is all set to tune it. Suddenly the violin is turned over to a rip saw-wielding, tone-deaf lumberjack." Colonel Walter Dornberger, *Der Schuss ins Weltall* (Esslingen: Bechtle, 1953).

6. James McGovern, later CIA station chief in Berlin, *Crossbow and Overcast* (New York: William Morrow, 1966).

7. Josef Goebbels, *Diaries for 1945* (Hamburg: Hoffman and Kampe, 1982).

8. Albert Speer, *Infiltration: The SS in the Armament Industry* (New York: Macmillan, 1982).

9. To a German at the time, the reference "Allies" meant, of course, the Four Powers.

10. Von Braun, at the head of a group of 120 Peenemunde designers, engineers, and technicians, accepted service contracts with the U.S. Air Force at an initial daily pay of six dollars and resumed research and rocket production at Fort Bliss. On April 15, 1950 they moved to Huntsville, Alabama, where forty-five of the original group still made their home in 1983. The group includes Bernard Tessmann, who with Dieter Huzel had concealed the archives and subsequently helped the United States in their recovery. Dornberger spent some two years in Britain as a prisoner of war before he was free. He later became consultant to Bell Aerospace in the United States.

11. The U.S. Strategic Bombing Survey Mission included Paul Nitze, chief U.S. negotiator in 1983 at the U.S.-Soviet talks at Geneva on the reduction of medium-range nuclear missiles. The 1945 mission also included John Kenneth Galbraith, George Ball, and Henry Alexander. The mission was headed by Franklin d'Olier.

12. Speer was arrested two days later. He subsequently served the full twenty-year sentence meted out by the International Military Tribunal at Nuremberg for war crimes. Speer was released from Spandau on October 1, 1966. He died in London on September 1, 1981, aged 76.

Chapter Six

1. The Reich Protectorate comprised the Czech provinces of Bohemia and Moravia, which was seized by the Third Reich after 1939 and classified as an "Appended Territory." In contrast, the Sudetenland was an area separated from Czechoslovakia under the 1938 Munich Treaty between Britain and Germany and had been formally incorporated into the Third Reich.

2. Up to one-half of the thirty-eight Waffen SS divisions fighting on the eastern front were made up of non-German volunteers: French, Dutch, Norwegian, Flemish, Walloon, Belgian, and Baltic troops, as well as the Vlasov Army of Russian ex-prisoners of war. These "ideological traitors" wore the regular gray-green Wehrmacht uniforms, with skull-and-crossbones cap insignia, black-collar patches, and distinctive piping on their epaulettes—blue for the French and yellow for the Walloons. In 1944, a formation of Belgian SS troops were rushed to Normandy from the eastern front to "defend" the German-occupied Continent against the "American and British invaders." It was a far cry from 1914, when countless Britons died defending Belgian independence after the German invasion of August 2, 1914. After World War II, thousands of Wehrmacht survivors joined the French Foreign Legion and served with distinction in Indo-China, much to the chagrin of some veteran Legionaires, who had felt that the Germans had upstaged their own military skills.

3. Charles Whiting, *Patton* (New York: Ballantine, 1970).

4. Charles B. MacDonald, *Last Offensive in the European Theatre of Operations* (Washington, D.C.: Office of the Chief of Military History, 1973).

5. General John R. Dean, *The Strange Alliance* (London: John Murray, 1947).

6. The U.S. Army newspaper. The group included Seymour Freiden, then with the *New York Herald Tribune* and now with Hearst Newspapers, John Groth, from *American Legion Magazine,* and others.

Chapter Seven

1. Under the terms of the 1943 Treaty of Friendship and Cooperation between the exiled Czechoslovak government in London and the Soviet Union and a subsequent 1944 agreement giving the Soviets the right to occupy all of Czechoslovakia after cessation of hostilities. Under the deal, which put Czechoslovakia into the Soviet orbit long before the German collapse, there were to be no U.S., British, or French zones, as in Germany and Austria.

2. Hitler had always been fascinated by Skoda. As early as 1923, he told his Harvard-educated, six-foot-four-inch foreign press chief and court jester Dr. Ernst Sedgwick (Putzi) Hanfstaengl, "We shall have to get these Skoda Works under German control one day." Hanfstaengl, who turned his back on Hitler in 1934 and spent most of the war years in the United States, was a schoolmate of SS Reichsleader Heinrich Himmler.

3. In 1968, in the wake of the attempt of Alexander Dubček, First Secretary of the Czechoslovak Communist Party, to introduce "Communism with a human face," several reforms, and an abolition of censorship, troops of the five Warsaw Pact states invaded Czechoslovakia in the face of passive resistance of the entire population. After tough negotiations, a state of "normalization" was reached, but censorship was reintroduced. The continued stationing of Russian troops in Czechoslovakia was negotiated soon after.

4. Assessment and partial investigation report on the Skoda Works, prepared for the British Combined Intelligence Objective Committee by Mission Chief Lieutenant Colonel James Brierly, Ordnance Department, and the British Intelligence Ordnance Survey Final Report, No. 43, on the Skoda Works, Pilsen, by H.G. Barber, Ministry of Supply, Visit of 22–25 September, 1945.

5. British technical intelligence experts rated Skoda's gear-cutting shop as "probably one of the most comprehensive in the World."

6. The subsequent Communist takeover of Czechoslovakia, facilitated by the fact that Prague was allowed to be taken by the Red Army in 1945, cemented the East-West Cold War in 1948. It shook the British government, which frankly admitted in secret cabinet papers (released in 1979) that once again it could do nothing but voice disapproval. When the takeover was complete in March 1948, Ernest Bevin, Foreign Secretary, told the cabinet that a "purge of the whole country is in progress, and all Western influences will shortly be suppressed."

Chapter Eight

1. Voss's refusal so angered Goering that he drew a pistol and threatened to have him arrested. Voss's aide-de-camp, *SS Obersturmbannführer* Albert Baudin prevented a shootout and managed to get Voss to his car through a back staircase. Voss related the incident to me in 1949. Some details were later filled in by a former Skoda executive.

2. The bronze lamp posts, designed by Speer, survived the war. The boulevard they now line has been renamed Strasse des 17 Juni, to commemorate the historic uprising of East German workers in 1953, the world's first mass revolt of the proletariat against Communist authority. The defiance and pelting of Red Army tanks by stone-throwing East Berlin youths, within sight of Free World newsreel cameras, stunned the Soviets and the East German People's Police on Potsdamer Platz, the East-West boundary.

3. Voss was also chairman of the administrative board of the Brünn Waffenwerke, which designed the Bren rapid-firing machine gun for the British Army shortly before World War II. He also held board or other senior posts in the Avia aircraft manufacturing firm of Prague, the Hermann Goering Weapons and Machine Construction Works, and other heavy engineering works.

4. Voss was unable to learn his name or his exact position on the U.S. team that had charge of the Skoda plant, pending its scheduled handover to the Red Army.

Chapter Nine

1. An investigation into the massacre was launched in 1953 by the public prosecutor of Arnsberg, Westphalia. The trial, covered by the author, took place in December 1957. All six accused entered pleas of not guilty on the grounds of having carried out "lawful" orders. Three of the six, including SS judge Wolfgang Wetzling, Judge Advocate of the Rocket Division, were found guilty.

2. The Waffen SS veterans organization HIAG *(Hilfsgemeinschaft für Gegenseitigreit)* is officially a mutual aid society that is affiliated with the General German Federation of Ex-Servicemen. The Bonn government has recently struck HIAG from the list of right extremist organizations.

3. The Prague region included Auschwitz, Cracow, Lublin, and Kattowitz.

4. The Vlasov Army was named after its commander, General Andrey Andreyevich Vlasov, defender of Moscow, who was taken prisoner by the Germans in July 1942. The Russian Army of Liberation under him consisted of Soviet prisoners of war, used as SS auxiliaries. Vlasov was one of the younger Red Army generals. Before the war he headed the Soviet Military mission to the Nationalist Chinese government of Chiang Kai-shek. After the end of hostilities, the United States handed over Vlasov and other officers of the Vlasov army to the Soviet Union. Vlasov was sentenced to death by a military tribunal and executed on August 12, 1945.

5. Likewise unlisted is SS General Heinrich Mueller, head of the Gestapo and second in command to Himmler. Mueller was last seen in the Chancellory bunker on April 29, 1945, the day before Hitler's suicide. Subsequently German officer prisoners of war in Russia reportedly saw him alive and active in Moscow, some years later. According to German intelligence reports, Mueller had slipped across the German border with forged papers. According to the reports, Mueller had ingratiated himself with the KGB during his handling of the investigation of the Soviet "Red Orchestra" espionage ring in Germany and had been suspected of having ties with the KGB.

6. J. Foltmann and H. Möller-Witten, *Opfergang der Generäle.* Berlin: Bernard & Graefe, 1953. Bernard & Graefe also published the war diaries of the German supreme command, covering 1940–1945.

Chapter Ten

1. Albert Speer, *Infiltration of the SS into the Armament Industry* (New York: Macmillan, 1982).

2. Under Allied agreements signed in London on August 8, 1945, War Criminals cannot claim to be free of responsibility for their crimes, even if they prove that they had acted under superior orders.

3. James McGovern, *Crossbow and Overcast* (New York: William Morrow, 1964).

4. During the opening session of the trials, Hans Fritsche, coordinator of German Radio, made a reference to Martin Bormann's attempt on the day Hitler committed suicide to contact the Soviets. Fritsche wrote, after his acquittal on all charges, that the issue was never pursued by the tribunal.

1. The Czechs did not try him. His release was sponsored by the general manager of the Brünn Waffenwerke, maker of the Bren gun, and personal letters from Skoda staffers. One of Voss's fellow detainees was Goering's half brother Albert, a fellow Skoda director and prewar production chief of the Tobis Film Studios in Vienna. And like Voss, Albert Goering was free without trial.

2. The top VIP of the group, Rudolf Hess, Hitler's deputy as party chief, was among them. Voss flew to England on a secret mission in May 1941 and spent the decisive war years in Britain. The secret British file that might explain why he flew to Britain will remain closed until the year 2020.

3. The Russians violently protested against the requested release of the Foreign Office documents, especially when the German defense gave notice that it would introduce the secret protocols of the Nazi-Soviet NonAggression Pact of 1939 (signed by von Ribbentrop and Molotov) under which Germany and the Soviet Union had agreed on the carving up of Poland (its fourth partition) and the rest of Eastern Europe, even before war broke out.

4. The key facts are contained in the summaries of six interrogations Voss underwent between December 11, 1946 and March 27, 1947. The reports were released to the author by the Imperial War Museum Archives in London. The summaries, prepared by the U.S. prosecution staff at Nuremberg, were written in very poor English. They followed the chronic German practice of omitting first names and initials, even at the first mention of the person. Retranslations, when English texts or testimonies were translated into German, then retranslated into English, often led to confusion and totally unrepresentative texts. The author recalls this from the time he covered the Nuremberg trials.

5. The same headquarters where SS Colonel Klaus Barbie, wartime Gestapo chief of Lyons, France, was hired as a U.S. intelligence undercover agent in 1947, to keep Communists and Nazis under surveillance. Barbie held the job until 1951, when the U.S. intelligence officers who had hired him, fearing exposure for using Barbie, smuggled him out to Bolivia under a false name. The ploy blew up in the laps of U.S. intelligence in 1983, when Barbie's cover was blown and he was extradited to France to stand trial.

6. The appeal keynoted an exclusive interview McCloy had granted International News Service general manager, Seymour Berkson, and the author.

FOOTNOTES

7. A secret service training operation was set up by former SS Colonel Otto Skorzeny, famous for his wartime exploits of infiltrating a commando unit dressed in U.S. Army uniforms into a U.S. Army column. In 1943 he engineered the dramatic rescue of deposed Italian dictator Benito Mussolini from a mountain fortress where he had been confined by the post-fascist Italian government.

8. To add fire to the media barbs, Schacht was discovered to be Colonel Skorzeny's father-in-law.

9. The breach and cancellation of industrialization-aid accords came in 1960.

10. *Gränze der Soviet Macht* (Würzburg: Hözner Publishing House, 1954), written in collaboration with a Göttingen University study group. The U.S. copyright was acquired by *U.S. News and World Report.* The serialization started in November 1955.

11. Defense counsel at Nuremberg for his father, pre-Hitler Chancellor Franz von Papen, who was acquitted by the International Military Tribunal.

Chapter Twelve

1. *Infiltration: The SS in German Armament* (New York: Macmillan, 1981).

2. Kammler not only set up the SS research operation at Pilsen, but as deputy to Paul Pleiger, head of the vast Hermann Goering Works, holding company for all mining and steel enterprises in the Reich, including Skoda, also had a very senior voice in this capacity.

3. Referred to under Section 190, *Atomic Shield,* the official history of the Atomic Energy Commission (Philadelphia: University of Pennsylvania Press, 1969).

4. Extract from the final report to U.S. Congress of the select committee, chaired by Representative Ray J. Madden of Indiana.

5. Quoted by the late James Agate, *London Sunday Times* critic and columnist, in his autobiographical *Ego 9.* London: 1948: George Harrys.

Index

INDEX

United Nations Charter, 113
United States, 8, 13, 32–34, 38–39,
    42, 57, 71, 74–75, 77–78, 82,
    104–5, 113–116, 120, 122–24,
    127–28, 143; intelligence, 71, 73,
    77, 86, 94, 105, 115, 120, 124–25,
    129; Freedom of Information Act,
    124, 130; Army, 43, 56–57, 60,
    63, 67, 71, 83, 88, 104, 106, 128,
    130–31; Navy, 39; zone of Ger-
    many, 21, 62, 67, 73, 83–85, 98
U.S. First Army, 60
U.S. Third Army, 6, 45, 63, 65, 69, 70,
    79; Third Armored Division, 16,
    27; Combat Command B (CCB),
    16, 27–30, 42, 65, 132, 138; 7th
    Army, 57; 9th Army, 68; Ninth
    Armored Division, 44; 16th Ar-
    mored Division, 63, 70; 44th Ar-
    mored Division, 57; Twelfth
    Army Group, 22
U.S. missile program, 105
U.S. National Archives, 59, 69, 129,
    131
U.S. Strategic Bombing Survey Mis-
    sion, 58–59
Uranium-235, 32, 37–38, 40

V-rocket terror, 5, 18, 59, 104, 127
V-1 bombs, 5, 28–29, 42, 44, 95, 127
V-2 rocket, 5–6, 8, 12, 17–18, 27–31,

    42–44, 47, 50, 55, 58, 95, 104,
    127–28
Van Vliet Report (Van Vliet), 130–31
VE Day (Victory Day in Europe), 80
Versailles Treaty, 14, 80, 133
Von Braun, Dr. Wernher, 8, 12, 42–
    43, 45–52, 57, 87, 95, 104–6, 123,
    128; arrest by Himmler, 50; con-
    tract with U.S., 58; surrender to
    U.S., 58
Voss, Dr. Wilhelm, 3ff., and secrets
    leakage, 94; and Skoda, 72–73,
    79, 82–83, 88–89, 112–113

War crimes, 4, 63, 89, 94, 105, 111,
    113, 128
Warsaw, 26, 43; Ghetto, 6, 9
Warsaw Pact, 107
Wartime Diary (Lindbergh), 28, 132,
    137
Washington, 29–30, 32–33, 57, 69, 74,
    77, 85, 115–16, 121–22, 128, 130,
    135
Wehrmacht, 24, 82, 86, 90, 117
Who's Who in Nazi Germany, 11
Wilhelmstrasse (Foreign Office), 113
World War I, 4, 28, 105
World War II, 27, 33, 35, 124, 126,
    130, 132, 142

Yalta, 15